AF439267

Resilience Is a Decision

Resilience is the structural consequence of decisions made before stress arrives.

RESILIENCE IS A DECISION

Resilience Is a Decision

A GOVERNANCE FRAMEWORK FOR SUSTAINING STRUCTURAL RESILIENCE

James M. Willis

InDev Strategic Press

RESILIENCE IS A DECISION

RESILIENCE IS A DECISION

Copyright © 2026 James M. Willis

All rights reserved.

No part of this publication may be reproduced, distributed, or transmitted in any form or by any means, including photocopying, recording, or other electronic or mechanical methods, without the prior written permission of the publisher, except in the case of brief quotations embodied in critical reviews and certain other noncommercial uses permitted by copyright law.

Published by InDev Strategic Press

ISBN: 979-8-9951649-0-6

First edition

To Jennifer and my family, without whom this work would not exist.

And to those entrusted to step up and step in.

RESILIENCE IS A DECISION

RESILIENCE IS A DECISION

PREFACE

In March of 1993, what became known as the Storm of the Century moved across the eastern United States. It wasn't a localized weather event. It was a multi-state disruption that hit infrastructure, transportation, communications, logistics, and public safety systems simultaneously.

The utility system I worked for took heavy damage. Poles were down, lines were compromised, and access routes were blocked across the entire operational territory. Crews mobilized, and assessments began as quickly as conditions allowed. The operational strain was significant, but it was within the impact parameters utilities understand as a severe weather event. They are built to respond to storms. What was unusual wasn't the local damage. It was the scale of the event itself.

Under ordinary circumstances, long-standing mutual aid agreements would have supplemented our response within hours. Equipment and personnel would be mobilized from neighboring systems. This reinforcement wasn't optimism. It was a standard operating reality.

This time, reinforcement didn't arrive. The same storm that hit us had hit them. It wasn't that our partners were unwilling; it was that their capacity to respond to mutual aid requests had collapsed under identical stress. We were on our own, operating inside a system designed on the assumption that help would come.

That moment clarified something that extended far beyond restoration logistics.

Mutual aid works. Until it doesn't.

There had been no failure of intent, no lapse in professionalism, no breakdown in relationships. The problem was shared exposure. What it revealed was a structural limitation, not a failure of capability. The redundancy we relied upon was not truly independent. When stress synchronized, response capacity compressed everywhere at once. The system fractured along its commonalities and failed in cascading sequence.

That realization has stayed with me long after power was restored.

This pattern of compression failure has recurred across every sector I've worked in, across industries and institutions, in developed and emerging economies, on multiple continents. The geography changed. The structural behavior did not. Hospitals depended on backup transfer agreements that shared the same transportation constraints they were designed to bypass. Supply chains buffered across multiple vendors that drew on the same upstream logistics corridors. Financial institutions distributed services and redundant systems across data centers that shared geographic and infrastructure pathways. The pattern even appeared in emergency evacuation plans, where multiple designated exit routes had been documented as alternatives, yet all funneled through the same corridors and escape channels. The alternatives existed on paper, but the independence did not.

The culprit isn't negligence. It's shared assumption.

Most organizations are built to perform reliably within expected conditions. They plan for disruption and respond to it with discipline. What they rarely examine is structural depth, specifically whether fallback systems actually survive the same stress that disabled the primary system.

Resilience, properly understood, isn't about predicting disruption or cataloging threats. It is about architectural integrity. When stress cascades across interconnected systems, the governing question isn't whether a system fails, but whether that failure becomes systemic. That outcome is determined by structure, not by the severity of the event.

That responsibility rests with governance. Boards and executive leaders don't govern storms, cyber intrusions, market contractions, or crisis. They govern the architectural and structural decisions that determine whether the organization absorbs the stress such events create or amplifies it. This requires a structural framework that forces that examination before disruption demands it.

The PACE Resilience Framework introduced in this book didn't originate in corporate governance; it originated in military communications planning, where the cost of getting it wrong is immediate, and the margin for error is zero. Military planners built the original PACE model around a simple but demanding principle: if your backup shares the same supporting systems as your primary communication channel, it isn't a backup; it's a redundancy. Under stress, it fails with the primary. That same discipline applies to how institutions are governed.

That same discipline extends into governance architecture, into how institutions design operational continuity, vendor ecosystems, digital platforms, capital access, authority pathways, and structural independence across tiers. The principle is the same regardless of sector or scale. Institutions endure or collapse based on structural decisions made before disruption applies compression.

When the Primary fails, what survives next, and why? Most organizations assume the answer without examining it. They have backups, continuity plans, and redundant systems. What they often lack is verification of independence across those layers. When stress synchronizes, that distinction stops being theoretical.

Cascade doesn't announce itself. It is the accumulating impact of progressive failures across systems that were assumed to be independent but were not. It surfaces quietly, through dependencies that routine reporting never identified or examined, and that stability never stressed or tested. That is a governance problem, not an operational one, and it requires a governance response before disruption forces the question.

PART I

Assumption and Exposure

Part I examines the condition that makes structural vulnerability possible in the first place: the assumption that performance proves resilience. Three chapters build the diagnostic foundation. The first examines how stability shapes interpretation and displaces examination. The second separates reliability from structural independence. The third identifies Correlation Risk, the hidden mechanism through which isolated failures become synchronized collapse. Together they describe the problem that the rest of the book is designed to address.

Stability is persuasive not because it guarantees durability, but because it reinforces the perception of control.

When systems perform reliably, when deliveries arrive on schedule, when financial metrics track within forecast and external scrutiny remains routine, leaders internalize continuity as evidence of sound structure. Performance becomes proof, and over time organizations begin to equate the absence of visible failure with the presence of structural independence, treating them as the same condition when in reality they are distinctly different.

The distinction is subtle but consequential. Systems can perform reliably for extended periods while sharing concentrated dependencies that remain dormant under ordinary conditions.

Exposure doesn't typically present itself as weakness. It accumulates through integration, quietly and incrementally, as each rational decision builds on the last without anyone examining the cumulative structural effect or the consequences each carries.

Modern institutions are becoming increasingly complex, interconnected, and infrastructure-dependent, and as that interconnection deepens, shared infrastructure becomes shared exposure. Efficiency, growth, and scale accelerate that progression. No single decision produces fragility, but the compounding effect of those decisions can compress insulation across tiers in ways that no individual decision was ever examined to prevent.

Few leaders deliberately ignore risk, but they consistently underestimate correlation and assume that structural integrity exists across their fallback systems without verification. They presume that if systems have not failed together before, they will not fail together under future stress. They mistakenly treat historical stability as a proxy for structural independence. Stability only confirms that conditions have not yet identified what structure cannot sustain. It does not confirm that independent structural resilience exists.

Until independence is demonstrated and exposure is located and mapped, resilience cannot be validated and fallback cannot be trusted. Stability does not eliminate vulnerability. It disguises it.

CHAPTER 1

When Stability Is Assumed

Think about the last major strategic initiative your organization approved. The business case was sound, performance metrics supported it, and integration improved efficiency. Every element aligned with the direction leadership had already committed to, and the decision moved forward with confidence.

The question nobody asked was whether that alignment was quietly compressing independence.

That's how stability shapes interpretation, not through negligence, but through the persuasive weight of things working. When processes align with strategy, when vendors align with procurement objectives, when infrastructure aligns with demand, alignment stops being examined because it appears to be the evidence of sound governance. Over time, it becomes the assumption that replaces examination.

That's where fragility forms. Not in the decisions that fail, but in the decisions that succeed so consistently that nobody looks beneath them.

Performance becomes proof over time, and that's where the problem quietly begins. Boards observe consistent metrics and interpret them as evidence of sound structure. Executives see targets met and infer durability. What hasn't failed is presumed stable.

What hasn't failed together is presumed independent. The longer that record holds, the more persuasive those presumptions become.

Stability shapes interpretation long before it shapes architecture. When systems perform reliably within anticipated variance, leaders internalize the boundaries of that variance as structural integrity. That's not a character flaw. It's how experienced people read patterns. The difficulty is that historical performance confirms what conditions have allowed, not what structure can sustain.

Leaders naturally project forward from historical success. If fallback layers performed in previous disruptions, they're presumed reliable for the next one. If reinforcement arrived when requested, it gets built into planning assumptions as a given rather than a variable. The stronger the performance record, the more persuasive that projection becomes, and the less likely that the underlying structure receives the depth of examination warranted.

That projection is where resilience stops being examined and starts being assumed. If independence across fallback tiers hasn't been examined, differentiated, and validated, resilience hasn't been chosen. It's drifted into place, and stability has made it look like a decision.

Governance must require that examination. Not as a crisis response, but as a standing discipline applied before performance history becomes the only evidence of structural integrity.

The Storm of the Century made this dynamic impossible to ignore. The planning model wasn't theoretical. It had been built from years of operational experience, and it had worked. What it hadn't been tested against was simultaneous external degradation across every system we depended on at once.

When the same stressor hit both our Primary system and the systems we relied on for continuity, the assumption of independence didn't bend. It collapsed. The mutual aid networks that proximity had made reliable under isolated disruption became unresponsive under synchronized stress for exactly the same reason they had seemed reliable: they were close, they were connected, and they shared our exposure.

The distinction matters. An attribute that strengthens performance under isolated disruption can compress survivability under synchronized disruption. Proximity isn't inherently a liability. But it becomes one when it's mistaken for independence through unvalidated integration.

Synchronized stress is under-modeled in most organizations for one straightforward reason: planning gravitates toward probable scenarios rather than compound convergence. It's a rational prioritization, but it creates a dangerous gap between what worst-case scenario planning looks at and what actually exists.

Consider the Titanic. The ship's compartmentalized hull design was genuinely innovative and genuinely sound under the scenarios it had been designed to survive. What it hadn't been designed for was a breach extending across multiple compartments simultaneously. Edward Wilding, one of Titanic's designers, testified at the British inquiry that the total cumulative hull damage was approximately 12 square feet, roughly the size of a typical household door.

The design wasn't flawed by negligence. It was validated against the wrong stress model.

The same pattern appeared in both the Challenger and Columbia disasters. In each case, the component that failed had a performance history and had survived previous missions. That survival record had been treated as design validation when it was actually something far narrower: confirmation that prior conditions hadn't yet demanded what the design couldn't provide. The distinction cost lives.

The structural logic is identical across sectors, industries, and scales of operation. A track record of survival under anticipated conditions isn't validation of structural integrity under compound stress. It's evidence that compound stress hasn't arrived yet.

That planning gap is reinforced by how most institutions are organized. Risk analysis follows functional boundaries, and those boundaries discourage the cross-domain examination that synchronized stress actually demands. Operations owns operational risk. Technology owns cyber risk. Procurement owns supply chain exposure. Finance owns liquidity. Each group performs its function, but nobody owns the interaction between them or the shared subsurface fragility that emerges under simultaneous stress, because neither appears on any organizational chart.

When those domains compress together, the consequences don't add up, they multiply. Infrastructure degradation narrows digital recovery options at the same time digital impairment slows restoration coordination. Transportation constraints limit workforce mobility precisely when operational demand is highest. Liquidity pressure tightens procurement flexibility when it's needed most. What might have been manageable in sequence becomes genuinely difficult in parallel, and difficult in parallel spirals into unmanageability under compressing decision velocity.

When fallback tiers share enabling inputs, leaders face narrowing options at accelerating speed. Without predefined differentiation, escalation becomes negotiation, and negotiation under pressure consumes the one resource that synchronized stress is already depleting: time.

Leaders who believed fallback capacity existed discover under compression that what they had was proximity, not independence. The options believed to be reliable and available were never structurally validated. They were inherited from the same exposure that disabled the Primary, making their failure under identical stress not a possibility but a structural certainty.

Differentiated options are what resilience actually provides. Not the absence of disruption, not a guarantee against failure, but the presence of viable pathways when disruption compounds. That distinction is architectural, and it has to be decided before the pressure arrives.

When fallback layers fail together, the organization is left with improvisation rather than architecture. Improvisation has succeeded before, which is precisely why it gets mistaken for a viable fallback. But improvisation under compressing decision velocity, degraded information, and simultaneous domain stress rarely holds, and when it fails the consequences compound faster than any improvised response can manage.

Delay and insulation are not the same protection, and stability makes it easy to confuse them. Delay buys time for stress to dissipate before shared dependencies collapse, and under isolated disruption that's typically enough. Insulation preserves survivability regardless of how long stress persists or how many domains it reaches. Stability masks that difference because delay is normally sufficient, and sufficient is where examination stops.

In calm conditions, governance seldom asks whether past endurance resulted from structural independence or simply from favorable conditions that weren't exhausted. That question typically surfaces for the first time under compression, when the answer is no longer actionable.

Stability can be proof of sound design. It can also be evidence that stress has not yet revealed correlation.

CHAPTER 2

Reliability Is Not Resilience

Here is a question worth putting to your board: when was the last time your organization distinguished between a system that performs reliably and a system that's structurally independent under stress? If the answer is that the question hasn't been asked, that gap is worth examining before disruption asks it for you.

Reliability is real and valuable. It reflects disciplined design, operational refinement, and sustained performance within expected conditions. For boards and executive leaders, strong reliability metrics provide legitimate reassurance that the enterprise is functioning as intended. The problem isn't that reliability is overvalued. It's that it's being used to answer a question it wasn't designed to answer.

Reliability measures how well a system performs within modeled assumptions. It doesn't measure what happens when those assumptions fail simultaneously across interconnected domains. The longer a system performs reliably, the more its operating conditions become internalized as permanent rather than conditional. That internalization is where structural exposure quietly accumulates.

Consider how optimization actually works inside a complex institution. Each efficiency gain rewards deeper integration, and deeper integration rewards further consolidation. Each step strengthens performance and deepens interdependence at the same time. No single decision in that progression is wrong. The cumulative effect, however, can compress insulation across tiers in ways that individual performance metrics never reveal and reliability dashboards never surface.

At the governance level, PACE functions as a structural reasoning model, not a data-driven one, and that distinction matters more than it might appear. Governance decisions have to be made before complete data exists and before you can observe how systems actually behave under stress. The exposure that matters most lives in the relationships between systems, not in how individual components perform, and those relationships don't show up in metrics. Data remains essential at the operational level, where it supports implementation and validation. But at the governance level, resilience is a structural judgment, not a measurement. What that judgment requires becomes clearer when you look at where reliable components and independent systems actually diverge, and that gap shows up in the same patterns repeatedly, regardless of sector or scale.

A backup generator may function flawlessly under every test condition. But if fuel delivery depends on the same constrained transportation corridor that supplies the primary grid, independence is limited regardless of how well the generator performs in isolation. The component is reliable. The system isn't independent.

An alternate supplier may meet every contractual obligation consistently. But if that supplier sources from the same upstream manufacturing cluster as the primary vendor, the exposure remains shared. Two contracts, one vulnerability.

A distributed data architecture may appear geographically separated on an infrastructure diagram. But if both environments depend on the same fiber backbone, insulation is incomplete regardless of how the diagram reads. Redundancy exists. Independence does not.

These aren't edge cases. They're the natural consequence of optimization proceeding without structural interrogation. Each decision that created these conditions was rational. The cumulative effect was concentration that only becomes visible under synchronized stress.

Delay and insulation are not the same protection, and the difference between them is the most consequential distinction in this book. Redundancy can delay failure and buy time under isolated disruption. That's valuable, and under normal conditions it's typically enough. Insulation prevents failure from cascading across systems. Delay is temporal, insulation is structural, and only deliberate governance examination produces the latter. Reliability doesn't get you there on its own.

Boards often interpret strong reliability metrics as evidence of resilience because performance continuity is visible and measurable. Structural insulation isn't. It requires examining where dependencies converge rather than where components duplicate. That examination is rarely prioritized during stability because it doesn't improve performance metrics and may reveal concentration that complicates ongoing optimization initiatives.

Yet without that examination, organizations risk strengthening the very dependencies that will compress under synchronized disruption. The most consequential mapping exercises are the ones that never happen because everything appears to be working.

When analysis stops at component performance, resilience is assumed rather than examined. Extending that analysis across enabling inputs, and asking how systems fail together rather than how components perform individually, is what makes resilience architectural rather than accidental. For a board with fiduciary responsibility for continuity, that's the difference between governing structure and governing appearances.

The question isn't whether the organization is reliable; that can be demonstrated through metrics. The question is whether the architecture holds when those metrics no longer apply. That requires a different examination entirely, one that metrics were never designed to provide.

CHAPTER 3

Correlation Risk: The Hidden Amplifier

Most enterprise risk frameworks are built around a sensible premise: catalog what could go wrong, assess the likelihood and impact of each risk, and build mitigation strategies around those assessments. It's a disciplined approach and it works well within its design boundaries. The problem isn't the framework. It's that the framework was designed to evaluate risks as discrete categories, and Correlation Risk doesn't behave that way.

Correlation Risk isn't about what could go wrong in isolation. It's about what fails together when stress synchronizes across systems that were presumed to be independent. That distinction is architectural, not categorical, and it doesn't appear in any risk register until stress makes it visible.

Consider how this plays out under a major regional disruption. Power infrastructure, digital scheduling systems, fuel distribution networks, supplier manufacturing hubs, and emergency transport capacity all perform reliably under normal conditions and even under isolated disruption. Each has been assessed. Each has mitigation strategies assigned. Each appears manageable on its own.

The picture changes when stress synchronizes across those same systems. A severe weather event disrupts power infrastructure. The digital systems dependent on that infrastructure begin to degrade. Fuel distribution, already constrained by the same weather event affecting transportation corridors, slows. Supplier manufacturing hubs in the same region reduce output. Emergency transport capacity, drawing from the same constrained fuel supply, narrows precisely when operational demand intensifies.

Nothing failed because mitigation was inadequate. Everything failed because the mitigation strategies shared the same enabling inputs as the systems they were designed to protect. This is what Correlation Risk actually describes. Not individual probability, but the structural coupling that turns isolated failures into cascade. It isn't the probability of a single failure. It's the structural condition that determines whether failures cascade or remain contained when stress synchronizes.

Traditional risk frameworks evaluate whether risks are likely and whether mitigation is sufficient. Correlation Risk asks a different question entirely: what fails together, and why?

That question shifts analysis from categories to architecture. It requires examining where infrastructure, vendors, digital systems, financial channels, and authority structures converge, not just where they duplicate. It requires looking beyond direct dependencies to the indirect ones that don't appear on any risk register because they've never failed before.

Indirect dependencies are often the most dangerous for exactly that reason. An organization may diversify vendors across two companies while both source from the same manufacturing region. A digital system may operate across separate facilities that share fiber routing through a single geographic corridor. Emergency response contracts may span multiple providers who rely on the same constrained logistics infrastructure. On paper, diversification appears sufficient. Structurally, concentration persists, and it persists invisibly until stress reveals it.

Correlation Risk doesn't imply that failure is inevitable. It identifies the pathways through which failure may cascade when stress synchronizes. That distinction matters directly to how governance should approach it, because the objective isn't to eliminate all shared dependencies. It's to understand where they exist, map them deliberately, and ensure that at least one critical fallback tier is insulated from them.

Cascade isn't a single event. It's a progressive structural condition. When tiers share enabling inputs, degradation in one accelerates degradation in the next. Decision velocity compresses. Information clarity degrades. Authority pathways narrow. The window for effective response contracts faster than the organization's capacity to respond expands. That progression rarely announces itself. It builds through accumulated integration that nobody examined for cross-domain consequence.

Correlation Risk stays hidden for so long because it requires cross-domain visibility that organizational structure actively discourages. As we established in the previous chapter, risk analysis follows functional boundaries. Each domain may manage its exposure competently. Correlation Risk lives between those domains, in the interaction of their dependencies under stress, and that interaction doesn't belong to any single function's oversight responsibility.

Surfacing it requires governance-level inquiry, the authority to ask questions that cross departmental boundaries and the willingness to confront concentration that was created through otherwise successful optimization. That can be uncomfortable. Optimization is rewarded and celebrated. Acknowledging that it may have introduced structural concentration feels like criticizing decisions that delivered real performance gains.

It isn't criticism. It's governance. The decision to optimize without mapping cross-domain dependency isn't reckless. It's expedient. It gets evaluated within the boundaries of immediate performance gain rather than full structural consequence. When correlation isn't surfaced at governance depth, integration decisions get made without complete visibility into how stress may synchronize across tiers. In those moments, resilience isn't deliberately traded away. It quietly erodes.

Correlation Risk is the hidden amplifier in complex systems. It determines whether redundancy provides insulation or delay, and whether disruption remains contained or becomes systemic. Before resilience architecture can be constructed, Correlation Risk must be located, mapped, and examined at the governance level. Until it is, resilience architecture rests on assumptions that synchronized stress will eventually test.

The same structural condition that produces cascade within an institution produces cascade across sectors when shared enabling inputs fail simultaneously. The sixteen U.S. critical infrastructure sectors, energy, communications, water, transportation, healthcare, financial services, and the rest, do not operate as isolated systems. They form an interconnected ecosystem supported by common dependencies: shared power grids, shared communications infrastructure, shared transportation corridors, shared IT platforms, and shared water systems. When one of those dependencies becomes unstable, several sectors can be affected at once, not because they made poor individual decisions, but because they share the same structural exposure.

For example, a ransomware attack against a logistics provider can affect healthcare deliveries, food distribution, fuel movement, and manufacturing inputs simultaneously. A power outage disables water treatment, telecommunications, hospitals, and financial transactions in parallel. A cyber compromise of a shared software platform reaches every operator running it, regardless of sector. The mechanism differs each time. The structural condition is identical: tiers that share enabling inputs fail together under synchronized stress.

This is why Correlation Risk is not only an institutional governance problem. It is a sector-level and national-level governance problem. The question a board should ask about its own architecture, do our fallback tiers share the same enabling inputs, is the same question sector risk managers should be asking about cross-sector dependency. The examination PACE requires at the institutional level applies directly at the ecosystem level. The framework scales because the structural problem doesn't change with the size of the system it inhabits. The same interconnected dependency architecture that makes critical infrastructure sectors vulnerable to cascade exists across every commercial and manufacturing sector as well. Supply chains, distribution networks, digital platforms, energy dependencies, and logistics corridors connect commercial enterprises to the same shared exposure pathways. The structural examination is the same. The governance obligation is the same.

That connection runs in both directions. Institutions that participate in sector-level information sharing contribute to the collective visibility that individual structural examination alone cannot produce. No single organization can map every dependency pathway across the ecosystem it operates within. But an institution that shares early detection of a supply chain disruption, a vendor compromise, or an emerging concentration point contributes to the structural awareness of every organization that depends on the same pathways. Collective resilience is built from individual governance discipline, and individual governance discipline is strengthened by the shared awareness that sector-level participation makes possible.

PART II

Architecture and Design

Part II moves from diagnosis to design. Identifying exposure is necessary. It isn't sufficient. This section introduces the PACE Resilience Framework, Primary, Alternate, Contingency, Emergency, and examines how it applies across governance architecture, operational continuity, and capital decisions. It begins with the framework's origins, then examines the Primary as the foundation all fallback planning rests on, then addresses what designing genuine independence actually requires.

Identifying exposure is a necessary first step, but it only establishes the baseline. Awareness alone isn't enough, deliberately designed architecture is required for resilience to exist.

Diagnosis without redesign leaves the organization exactly where it was, only now it's aware of the vulnerability and structurally unchanged.

Resilience has to be engineered, and that's a harder requirement than it sounds. Updating risk registers, expanding dashboards, and producing additional contingency documentation all improve visibility without altering a single structural dependency. Visibility and structural independence are not the same condition, and improving one does not advance the other.

Structural independence requires deliberate differentiation. If fallback layers inherit the same infrastructure, vendor ecosystems, digital backbones, financial pathways, or authority structures as the Primary, architecture remains coupled regardless of how well the exposure has been mapped. Mapping tells you where the problem is. Design determines whether it gets resolved.

This is also where governance earns its weight. Boards and executive leaders don't build systems or select vendors. But they authorize capital, approve modernization initiatives, and set strategic direction. Every one of those decisions either concentrates or differentiates structural exposure. When governance doesn't require that examination, concentration accumulates by default, because efficiency always will, and differentiation requires a deliberate counterforce.

The framework introduced in this section doesn't replace existing risk management disciplines. Enterprise Risk Management catalogs exposure and assigns mitigation across categories. That function remains essential. What architecture governs is how exposure behaves when mitigation is insufficient, and whether the institution retains viable options when stress extends beyond what mitigation was designed to handle.

That is a different question from the ones ERM was built to answer, and it requires a different discipline to address it. That discipline is PACE, Primary, Alternate, Contingency, Emergency, and its logic is straightforward even where its application is demanding.

CHAPTER 4

Structured Fallback

The PACE Discipline and Its Governance Expansion

The PACE framework didn't begin in a boardroom. It began in operational environments where communication failure doesn't produce a service disruption. It produces a mission failure. Military planners developed Primary, Alternate, Contingency, Emergency to ensure that communication survives when situations degrade, when the preferred channel fails, when the backup is compromised, and when conditions deteriorate beyond what planning assumed. The driving principle wasn't elegance. It was survivability.

That principle is direct in its logic and unforgiving in its application: every communication pathway must be sufficiently different in its enabling inputs that the stressor affecting the Primary doesn't automatically compromise the Alternate. Proximity, shared infrastructure, common power sources, and geographic overlap all represent coupling that synchronized stress will exploit. Independence isn't assumed. It's verified.

The four tiers reflect a deliberate logic.

Primary represents the preferred pathway under normal conditions. It's optimized for efficiency and clarity, typically the most capable and most complex layer in the architecture.

Alternate provides a secondary pathway when the Primary fails. It isn't a duplicate. It must differ sufficiently in its enabling inputs that whatever stressed the Primary doesn't automatically stress the Alternate. It retains capability but carries less complexity than the Primary.

Contingency represents a further degraded but viable pathway when both Primary and Alternate are compromised. It's less efficient, may require manual workarounds, and is rarely elegant. It exists to preserve core function, not comfort.

Emergency represents the final viable pathway when everything else has failed. It may be slower, less capable, and less convenient. Its robustness comes from its simplicity and from the fact that it shares as few enabling inputs as possible with the tiers above it.

What makes this architecture work isn't the labels. It's the insistence that each tier fail differently from the one above it. If they don't, redundancy is superficial. Under stress, the backup fails with the Primary, and the architecture collapses to a single point of failure wearing the appearance of depth.

PACE doesn't eliminate failure. It prevents cascade. Those aren't the same outcome, and the difference between them is what governance is actually responsible for.

Every institution already has these four tiers whether they've been deliberately designed or not. The question is whether they've been differentiated. When governance doesn't mandate that differentiation, tiers remain structurally ambiguous. Under compression, undifferentiated layers collapse together because independence was never formally required and never structurally verified.

Every system operates within tolerance. There's a normal operating range where performance is optimized. There's an elevated range where stress can be absorbed temporarily without systemic consequence. Beyond that lies structural failure. The existence of fallback tiers reflects this reality. If resilience required only that a backup function as expected, a single Alternate would suffice. Multiple tiers exist because stress escalates and compression compounds.

As pressure increases, systems don't simply fail. They compress. Time narrows. Information clarity degrades. Authority concentrates. Shared dependencies surface. Enabling inputs that appeared independent reveal commonality. When tolerance thresholds are exceeded, degradation accelerates across interconnected domains simultaneously.

PACE doesn't verify that individual components function. It validates whether outcomes remain survivable under escalating compression. Primary architecture is optimized for performance within normal tolerance. Alternate architecture must be sufficiently insulated to function when those limits are exceeded. Contingency simplifies further, preserving essential mission while reducing dependency density. Emergency posture represents the final containment tier, concentrating authority and preserving core institutional function when layered stress threatens systemic stability.

As architecture descends from Primary to Emergency, dependency density narrows by design and survivability focus intensifies with each tier. Robustness at the lower tiers isn't duplication. It's differentiation under stress. When tiers inherit the same enabling inputs, they share the same tolerance limits and fail together under compression. That condition isn't resilience. It's the appearance of resilience.

This is where the PACE framework extends beyond its military communications origins into governance architecture. The core insight, that survivability depends on tier differentiation, applies across operational architecture, vendor ecosystems, infrastructure design, digital platforms, capital access, authority pathways, and institutional continuity. Organizations operating across layered systems face the same structural problem the military planners were solving: systems that appear separate may share enabling inputs. Under stable conditions those shared inputs remain invisible. Under synchronized stress they become the common fault line.

Translating PACE into governance requires understanding what governance is actually being asked to do. Boards and executive leaders aren't being asked to design communication pathways or select backup generators. They're being asked to ensure that the institution's architecture has been examined for tier differentiation, that independence has been verified rather than assumed, and that structural integrity is revalidated as the institution evolves.

That is a governance obligation, not an operational preference.

For boards, PACE provides a structural lens for evaluating whether advancement strengthens performance without silently compressing independence. Every modernization initiative, vendor consolidation, digital integration, or capital restructuring shifts exposure somewhere. The oversight question PACE structures is direct: does this initiative introduce correlated exposure across tiers that will amplify disruption under synchronized stress?

Executive leadership applies PACE as a failsafe discipline. It clarifies how the organization operates under stability, how continuity is sustained when the Primary degrades, what simplified posture preserves core mission when conditions deteriorate further, and what survivability stance concentrates authority when systemic stress threatens institutional viability.

At the operational level, PACE becomes concrete design. It shapes infrastructure segmentation, vendor diversification that accounts for upstream dependency, digital separation and manual workarounds, fleet composition and mobility strategy, authority delegation under degraded conditions, and what gets preserved when operations must intentionally degrade.

PACE doesn't compete with Enterprise Risk Management, business continuity planning, or operational risk oversight. Those disciplines remain essential. ERM catalogs exposure and tracks mitigation across categories. Business continuity planning documents procedural response. Crisis management defines activation and communication structures. Each addresses risk from its proper vantage point.

PACE operates at a different structural layer. Where ERM asks what could go wrong, PACE asks what is structurally coupled across tiers. It examines how domains interact when stress synchronizes and whether those interactions compress independence. It considers whether continuity plans are built on infrastructure that's structurally coupled. It evaluates whether authority pathways remain clear when multiple risk categories converge simultaneously.

The objective isn't to replace those frameworks. It's to ensure that when they perform well individually, they also function coherently under systemic stress, and that none of them unintentionally compress independence across tiers through shared architecture.

PACE is versatile because it is not domain-specific. It applies to any situation where layered systems must remain viable under stress, and anywhere the cost of cascade exceeds the cost of deliberate differentiation. When applied as a discipline, it reduces systemic risk and preserves structural adaptability. That application begins with an honest examination of the Primary, because the Primary is where exposure accumulates most quietly and where most governance examinations stop too soon. PACE doesn't eliminate failure. It changes what stands when failure arrives.

CHAPTER 5

Begin with the Primary

Where Exposure Actually Lives

Most organizations spend considerable energy designing fallback. Continuity plans are written, Alternates are documented, emergency authorities are defined, and business continuity binders are updated and reviewed. That work matters. But it rests on an assumption that rarely gets examined with the same rigor: that the Primary architecture itself is structurally sound.

It often isn't. Not because of negligence, but because the Primary evolves quietly while attention is directed elsewhere.

The Primary isn't a single system. It's the integrated architecture through which the organization performs during stability, the infrastructure, digital platforms, vendor ecosystems, capital structure, governance pathways, logistics corridors, authority chains, mobility assets, storage practices, maintenance procedures, and operational assumptions that combine to make normal performance possible. It changes rarely through dramatic redesign. It changes almost constantly through incremental advancement, and that's where exposure accumulates.

Organizations modernize systems. They integrate platforms. They centralize oversight. They consolidate vendors. They streamline logistics. They digitize workflows. They co-locate infrastructure for efficiency. Each decision is rational. Each strengthens performance under stable conditions. Each also shifts exposure in ways that don't show up in performance metrics and don't trigger governance review because no single decision crosses the threshold that would require it.

That's the structural inflection point. Advancement isn't neutral. It doesn't merely improve performance. It reshapes dependency architecture, and dependency architecture is what determines whether the Primary can sustain the stress that fallback planning assumes it can absorb.

Consider a remote water desalination facility serving as the sole freshwater source for an island population. It's a useful illustration precisely because the decisions made there are the same decisions being made in hospitals, financial institutions, manufacturing facilities, and digital infrastructure environments every day, just with more visible consequence.

The facility's control systems are digitized for efficiency, a sound decision that improves monitoring and reduces manual error. Replacement components are stored adjacent to operating units to accelerate maintenance response, a sound decision that reduces downtime. The vehicle fleet is transitioned to renewable energy to capture economic and environmental benefits, a sound decision that reduces fuel costs and emissions. Power supply is centralized to improve oversight and reduce redundancy, a sound decision that simplifies operations.

Each decision reflects sound reasoning. None of them, examined individually, would raise a governance concern. Examined collectively, they tell a different story.

If control systems and spare components are co-located, a single environmental event affects both simultaneously. Contamination, physical damage, targeted disruption, it doesn't matter which. The redundancy built into storing spares on site disappears the moment the site itself is compromised. If operational assets depend exclusively on centralized electrical supply and that supply is impaired during a crisis, response capacity narrows precisely when restoration demand is highest. If the same energy source powers both production and mobility, any impairment of that source compounds operational strain across every function simultaneously.

The modernization wasn't flawed. The concentration was unexamined. Each decision strengthened performance within its own domain. Nobody examined the cumulative structural effect across domains, or the consequences each decision carried for the tiers that were supposed to survive Primary failure.

That pattern repeats across sectors. Organizations centralize data environments to increase analytical capability. They reduce vendor redundancy to increase negotiating leverage. They streamline logistics to eliminate inefficiency. They pursue modernization to remain competitive. Each initiative is defensible on its own terms. Collectively, they can narrow the survivability pathways that fallback planning assumes will remain open.

This is where PACE functions as architectural discipline rather than contingency planning. Before designing Alternates or Contingencies, governance must examine the Primary honestly. Where is concentration increasing? Which geographic clusters carry disproportionate weight? Which vendor relationships share upstream exposure? Which digital integrations centralize control across multiple functions? Which authority pathways compress decision-making into fewer nodes? Which capital channels carry assumptions that haven't been stress-tested?

These aren't defensive questions. They're strategic ones. If the Primary accumulates concentration silently, fallback tiers will inherit it unless deliberately differentiated. Resilience can't be layered on top of unexamined coupling. It has to begin at the foundation, and the foundation is the Primary.

Seeing exposure clearly is the necessary first step. But clarity without structural response leaves the organization in exactly the position the Part II introduction described: aware of the problem and architecturally unchanged. The integrity of every fallback tier depends on how honestly the Primary has been examined and how deliberately what that examination reveals has been addressed.

CHAPTER 6

Designing for Independence

The concentration conundrum is that it's rarely introduced through negligence, but through success, and that's precisely what makes it difficult to confront. By the time leadership can clearly see it, the organization has usually already benefited from it. Integration reduced friction, consolidation improved margin, standardization simplified execution, and centralization strengthened oversight. Those outcomes are real. The structural consequence accumulated alongside them, quietly and without triggering any threshold that would have required governance review.

The film Margin Call illustrates this dynamic with uncomfortable precision. The firm's concentrated position in mortgage-backed securities wasn't built through recklessness. It was built through decisions that each delivered measurable performance gains. The concentration was the source of the returns. That's what made it so difficult to confront when the risk analyst's model revealed that the underlying assumptions had already failed. By the time the numbers were visible, unwinding the position would itself trigger the collapse it was meant to prevent.

Designing independence isn't about building duplicates. It's about ensuring that when stress synchronizes, the organization has options that remain viable. It means making certain that the

Alternate doesn't collapse with the Primary, that Contingency isn't merely the Primary under strain, and that Emergency posture doesn't rely on improvisation when decision velocity is already compressing. That requires a discipline stronger than aspiration and more durable than documentation.

The Structural Discipline Continuum describes how modern systems behave as they advance, why institutions often experience not a single failure but a sequence of failures that accelerate, compound, and propagate, and how the opposite can be engineered so that stress remains contained and recovery remains structurally achievable. It begins with a condition every advancing institution eventually faces: advancement always alters exposure.

When systems advance, capability increases, but dependency patterns shift. Digital integration improves coordination while introducing shared platforms. Vendor consolidation increases negotiating leverage while concentrating upstream exposure. Geographic clustering reduces logistics cost while narrowing independence. Electrification reduces fuel dependency while tying mobility to the reliability of electrical infrastructure. None of these advancements are inherently flawed. Many are necessary. The point isn't to resist modernization. It's to govern its structural consequence.

Exposure shift is what happens when improvement changes what the organization depends on, where it depends, and how many systems now rely on the same enabling inputs. It rarely appears in dashboards, which measure performance outcomes rather than dependency structure. Uptime doesn't reveal upstream coupling any more than margin improvement reveals corridor concentration. A successful modernization program doesn't, by itself, confirm structural insulation.

Exposure shift becomes concentration when it accumulates. Concentration isn't a moral failure or a leadership deficiency. It's a structural condition that emerges when multiple systems, or multiple fallback tiers, converge on the same enabling input. That enabling input may be energy, geography, logistics, digital infrastructure, vendor ecosystems, authority pathways, or capital access. It develops gradually because each contributing decision can be justified individually. Over time the organization begins treating concentration as normal because it's efficient and it works, until stress synchronizes.

Cascading vulnerability emerges here. Not as a dramatic collapse but as progressive compression. One impairment alters operating conditions for adjacent systems. Those systems degrade. Recovery pathways narrow. Decision cycles shorten. The organization begins consuming its own resilience faster than it can restore it.

The Structural Discipline Continuum describes this progression and interrupts it through deliberate differentiation.

Differentiation is the deliberate act of ensuring that critical tiers don't share the same enabling inputs. It isn't duplication for comfort. It's separation for survivability, achieved through geography, infrastructure, vendor ecosystems, power supply, digital segmentation, stock positioning, governance thresholds, or authority delegation. The method varies by context. The intent doesn't vary at all.

What differentiation produces when stress arrives is containment, the condition in which failure doesn't propagate freely and impairment doesn't automatically become systemic. In governance terms, containment is the difference between a difficult event and an institutional crisis, and it's the first structural outcome that makes everything else possible.

Containment makes recoverability achievable. Recoverability isn't restoration speed alone. It's the structural possibility of restoration under ongoing impairment, the ability to continue functioning while repairing, to operate in degraded posture without consuming the resources required for recovery.

Recoverability sustained over time becomes sustainability, the ability to carry commitments without relying on continuous heroics. That's what transforms resilience from a crisis story into a governance standard, and a governance standard is what makes structural discipline durable rather than episodic.

Consider the water production example from Chapter 5. A centralized control system improves efficiency and visibility. Replacement components are stored on site to reduce downtime. From a reliability standpoint, the system appears prepared. But resilience asks a different question: do the spares survive the same stress that impairs the Primary? If replacement components are stored adjacent to the operational system, environmental damage or targeted disruption may impair both simultaneously. The organization believes it has redundancy. It has built parallel vulnerability.

The same logic applies to fleet electrification. Sustainability goals advance. Operating costs decline. Maintenance simplifies. Yet mobility becomes dependent on the same constrained electrical infrastructure that powers production. Under grid impairment, response capacity narrows precisely when operational demand intensifies. The decision to modernize was rational. The exposure shift wasn't structurally evaluated. Differentiation doesn't require reversal. It requires segmentation. A Contingency mobility tier insulated from grid dependency preserves maneuverability without undermining modernization objectives.

Simplicity at the lower tiers isn't a design limitation. It's a structural requirement. Complex systems trend toward integration, and integration improves performance but increases coupling. Contingency must intentionally reverse that density. It clarifies what must continue at all costs, which processes can degrade to manual execution, and which functions can pause without systemic harm. Emergency posture narrows further still. Authority concentrates. Communication simplifies. Capital access becomes predefined rather than negotiated. Emergency architecture isn't improvisation. It's disciplined contraction defined before compression accelerates.

Some leaders view redundancy as waste. In some cases, duplication that shares enabling inputs does increase cost without increasing resilience. But removing redundancy without evaluating its structural role isn't prudence. It's exposure compression, and PACE exists to prevent that compression from occurring without governance awareness. It doesn't replace Enterprise Risk Management.

ERM catalogs exposures and tracks mitigation. PACE tests whether tiers fail differently when stress synchronizes. ERM confirms that risks are identified and tracked. PACE confirms that independence is preserved across the tiers those risks affect.

Boards approve strategies, capital plans, modernization programs, and public commitments. When hidden concentration causes those commitments to fail under stress, the institution experiences more than operational disruption. The boardroom scene in Margin Call captures this moment with uncomfortable accuracy. Jeremy Irons' character doesn't ask how the concentration was built. He asks what it will cost to unwind it, and Kevin Spacey's character has to explain that every available option triggers the collapse it was meant to prevent. The numbers are visible. The options are gone. That's what hidden concentration looks like when stress finally surfaces it. For the institution, the consequence is the same: credibility implosion, and credibility lost under visible, avoidable failure is far harder to restore than the systems that failed.

That's what structural discipline ultimately protects. Stakeholders, regulators, investors, and communities extend trust to leadership before disruption occurs. They withdraw it when disruption reveals that architecture was assumed rather than governed. Structural discipline is what keeps that from happening.

PART III

Governance and Endurance

Architecture determines survivability, but architecture alone doesn't sustain it. That's the responsibility governance carries, and it's the distinction Part III addresses directly.

Parts I and II established what structural resilience requires: honest examination of the Primary, deliberate differentiation across tiers, and disciplined interrogation of how systems fail together under synchronized stress. That work is necessary. It isn't sufficient on its own.

Architecture can be designed and still erode. Tiers can be differentiated and still converge over time as modernization, consolidation, and integration proceed without revalidation. Independence can be verified at one point in time and quietly compromised by the next capital cycle. Structural discipline doesn't persist automatically. It persists because governance requires it to.

What governance owns isn't crisis management, operational response, or continuity planning. Those disciplines matter, but they belong in the hands of the people who execute them. What belongs at the governance level are the structural decisions that determine whether the organization retains viable options when those disciplines are put to the test.

Boards and executive leaders make those decisions constantly, often without recognizing them as structural decisions. A capital allocation removes redundancy. A modernization initiative centralizes a previously distributed function and quietly compresses the insulation that distribution provided. A vendor consolidation narrows upstream diversity without appearing on any risk register. A digital integration unifies previously segmented platforms in ways that performance dashboards confirm as improvements while structural independence erodes beneath them. Each decision is evaluated for performance benefit, financial return, and strategic alignment. Structural consequence is rarely part of the evaluation unless governance requires it.

Concentration accumulates not through negligence but through the natural momentum of institutions doing what institutions do: optimizing for performance, efficiency, and scale under stable conditions, without examining what those optimizations do to structural independence under stress.

Part III examines how structured resilience protects leadership credibility when decisions are scrutinized under strain, how escalation authority must be defined before stress compresses decision velocity, and how the PACE Resilience Framework must be institutionalized across planning, procurement, capital allocation, and executive alignment to remain viable as organizations evolve.

Resilience that exists only in architecture diagrams doesn't endure. Governance is what makes it durable, and that durability has to be built into the same oversight structures that govern capital, strategy, and performance, not treated as a separate discipline that operates alongside them. The chapters that follow examine how governance behaves under stress, how structural discipline is embedded rather than invoked, how material decisions are audited for structural consequence, and what stewardship across leadership generations actually requires.

CHAPTER 7

Governing Under Stress

Failure is visible. Resilience isn't, and that asymmetry shapes how governance behaves during stability in ways that create real structural risk.

When systems absorb disruption without consequence, leadership takes it as confirmation that the architecture is sufficient. What looks redundant gets streamlined. What looks cautious gets questioned. Structural discipline that works produces no headline and no visible return. It preserves normalcy, and normalcy gets attributed to sound management rather than sound architecture. Under isolated disruption that pattern holds. The organization is strained but recognizable, and leadership confirms what it already believed.

Under compounded stress, the environment shifts in ways that isolated disruption never reveals. Physical damage overlaps with digital impairment, workforce fatigue arrives alongside public scrutiny, and liquidity strain tightens precisely when operational demands are highest. Information arrives rapidly, often incomplete and sometimes contradictory, as communication channels saturate and time compresses. The tempo accelerates faster than clarity forms.

What matters in those moments isn't what leadership does. It's what the architecture allows them to do. If fallback tiers are genuinely differentiated, leaders have options. If they aren't, leaders have improvisation, and improvisation under compressing decision velocity, degraded information, and simultaneous domain stress rarely holds.

Human judgment under compression is worth understanding because it explains why architecture matters more than confidence. Leaders don't evaluate information in isolation. They begin with assumptions because assumptions provide orientation. Without them, analysis collapses into noise. Under stable conditions, that works well. Experienced leaders read patterns accurately because the patterns have been reliable.

Under stress, the same cognitive process that produces good judgment during stability can limit it during compression. Information flows faster than it can be verified. Consequences accelerate before options can be fully evaluated. The mind gravitates toward established narratives because those narratives have previously produced stability, which means alternative interpretations narrow and option pathways appear fewer than they actually are. Leaders may hesitate not from fear but from the genuine difficulty of evaluating degraded information against compressed time with authority structures that were never stress-tested.

The cognitive mechanism behind this condition has been studied with particular rigor in intelligence analysis, where the consequences of compromised judgment are immediate and the documentation of how it fails is unusually precise. Richards J. Heuer Jr., writing for the CIA's Center for the Study of Intelligence, identified anchoring bias as one of the most persistent cognitive traps in analytical work under pressure. The first plausible explanation becomes the governing frame. From that point forward, new information is no longer evaluated independently against the full body of evidence. It is received through the anchor, recruited if it confirms the early judgment, explained away if it does not.

Heuer's central finding was that experienced analysts are not immune to this condition. Experience provides the pattern recognition that creates the anchor in the first place. The mind that has seen this before knows what it is looking at, and that certainty can close analysis at exactly the moment analysis most needs to remain open.

What makes anchoring bias structurally dangerous in governance terms is what happens when decision layers lack genuine insulation from one another. In a well-differentiated architecture, each tier evaluates the situation independently. The anchor formed at one level is interrupted rather than inherited by the level above it. Fresh analysis becomes structurally required at each escalation point.

When insulation is absent, the anchor propagates. The frame formed at the technical layer becomes the context in which the management layer receives the same information. The management layer's confirmation of that frame becomes the operating reality within which the authority layer above it deliberates. Each tier that should provide independent assessment instead imports the previous tier's conclusion. The bias moves upward unopposed, not because the people at each level are incapable, but because the architecture gave them no structural requirement to evaluate the situation fresh.

I have observed this directly in intelligence analysis contexts, including in the Solomon Islands environment described later in this book, and in other engagements across multiple continents, some of which I am not at liberty to describe in detail. In each case the condition was the same: an anchor formed early, insulation between decision layers was insufficient to interrupt it, and the architecture allowed a protected conclusion to move through the organization rather than being caught and corrected at an independent tier. The cognitive compression Heuer described is not specific to intelligence work. It operates in any decision architecture where the layers are not genuinely insulated from one another.

The PACE Resilience Framework compensates for that compression structurally, rather than asking leaders to perform differently under impossible conditions. By requiring deliberate interrogation of tier independence before stress arrives, PACE shifts evaluation away from narrative continuity and toward structural validation. The question stops being "Do we believe this will hold?" and becomes "Does this fail differently?" That shift is subtle in calm conditions and decisive under compression.

Architecture introduces disciplined friction against premature closure. It restores visibility of alternative pathways before stress makes them urgent. It doesn't remove the difficulty of governing under compression. It removes the ambiguity about how that compression should be managed, and ambiguity under synchronized stress amplifies cascade more reliably than disruption itself.

Consider how this plays out in a boardroom reviewing a major modernization initiative. The proposal is well developed and the business case is sound. Performance metrics are strong. Leadership confidence is high because similar efforts have succeeded before. The first layer of evaluation centers on expected performance gains, financial return, regulatory alignment, and implementation timeline. That evaluation is necessary, and it isn't sufficient.

A director asks a different question: if this becomes part of our Primary architecture, what enabling inputs does it concentrate? The tone shifts. Management explains the integration pathways: digital systems converging, vendor relationships consolidating, infrastructure nodes simplifying, oversight centralizing. Each decision strengthens efficiency. The director continues: if the Primary layer is impaired, what's the Alternate that fails differently?

Reassurance follows. There are backups, vendor commitments, and response protocols. The director presses further: does the Alternate rely on the same digital backbone, the same vendor ecosystem, the same infrastructure corridor? Redundancy exists. Independence is less certain. A third question follows: if both Primary and Alternate are impaired under synchronized stress, what Contingency posture preserves core mission? What degrades intentionally? What continues? Which enabling inputs must be segmented to preserve survivability? And finally: if escalation accelerates, who holds authority, and what capital mechanisms remain insulated from operational strain?

No accusation is made. No psychological correction is attempted. Structural interrogation replaces narrative comfort. The conversation shifts from "Will this work?" to "How does this fail?" and from "Do we have backup?" to "Does it fail differently?"

This is governance discipline applied before decisions harden into architecture, not invoked after disruption has already begun.

Boards are responsible for organizational integrity and structural prudence, and that responsibility becomes most visible after disruption subsides. Scrutiny rarely centers on whether the event occurred. It centers on whether leadership constructed architecture capable of anticipating correlated impairment.

Stakeholders don't expect omniscience. They expect evidence that governance examined the architecture deliberately: that concentration risk was mapped rather than assumed away, that escalation thresholds were defined in advance, and that capital exposure was modeled under compounded stress rather than isolated scenarios. If that examination can be demonstrated, governance posture remains defensible even when outcomes are imperfect. If it can't, execution competence becomes secondary to architectural omission.

That's not a legal argument. It's a leadership reality. PACE addresses it directly by providing evidence of structural discipline, demonstrating that survivability was not assumed but architected, mandated, and reinforced before disruption demanded proof.

Every modernization, consolidation, integration, or efficiency gain shifts exposure somewhere, and those shifts accumulate whether or not governance examines them. When those shifts aren't examined structurally, independence compresses quietly across tiers. Performance may improve while survivability narrows. An organization can become more capable and more fragile at the same time, and never know it until stress synchronizes.

The boardroom scenario describes governance functioning as it should, structural interrogation applied during stability before a decision hardens into architecture. That is the ideal version. It is worth holding alongside what actually happens when that examination hasn't occurred and stress arrives faster than any activation sequence can respond.

When the Architecture Is Actually Tested

In March 1993, what meteorologists called explosive cyclogenesis moved across the eastern United States. The system developed from spawn to landfall in under 24 hours. In southwest Georgia, it arrived without a development stage, a massive squall line driving hurricane-force winds across the region in a matter of hours, delivering full destructive force before any restoration doctrine could engage. There was no warning curve to read. There was no progressive signal to act on. The storm arrived complete.

Every utility in the region operated from the same informal architecture, built from decades of operational experience and never written down because it had never needed to be. Primary was internal, company crews and contractors already on the ground.

Alternate was regional, neighboring utilities and contractors available for supplemental support. Contingency was the formal mutual aid network, activated when damage exceeded internal and regional capacity, typically with some forewarning of what was approaching. Emergency didn't exist. Nothing in the operational history had ever demanded it.

That model was sound. It had worked. What it contained, without anyone having examined it, was a single hidden assumption: that warning time would exist before activation was required.

Every prior storm had provided enough forewarning to allow sequential escalation. The standard restoration approach was clear: work the early damage during the development stage, pull crews back to secure locations as conditions approached futility, redeploy as the storm subsided. Each phase was observable and created a window for the next decision. The activation decisions mapped to conditions that arrived progressively and could be read in real time. The model had never been written down because it had never been tested against a storm that didn't behave that way.

Explosive cyclogenesis doesn't arrive progressively. There is no development stage to work. The pull-back threshold is designed to be read as wind speed and damage rate increase, conditions that in a normal storm arrive with enough separation to allow a decision. This storm delivered those conditions simultaneously and at full intensity. By the time the Alternate could have been formally activated, it was already unavailable. By the time the Contingency should have been triggered, the same storm had moved through every region those mutual aid networks covered, leaving them in the same condition we were in.

The redundancy was real. The independence was not.

The system I managed produced 100 percent customer disruption. Ninety percent of the physical system required some level of restoration, not uniform catastrophic failure, but a territory-wide mosaic of downed lines, compromised equipment, and debris and limbs on wires, each situation requiring individual assessment and sequenced response across a system the storm had reached simultaneously. When conditions allowed work to begin, I wasn't executing a pre-designed Emergency response. I was building one from what was at hand: paper maps, two-way radios, a makeshift war room, senior staff distributed across sections of the territory to provide the situational clarity that restoration sequencing required. The command structure that should have been pre-designed had to be constructed in the first operational window after the storm passed, consuming hours that should have been spent on restoration.

It held. That's the part worth being direct about. Within 72 hours we had restored enough of the system to cut crews loose and begin lending assistance to neighboring utilities still consumed by their own response. The improvised command structure worked. The distributed senior staff managed their sections. Restoration outpaced what a territory-wide damage footprint of that scale would normally suggest was possible. But operational isn't the same as restored. Significant repairs remained, and makeshift solutions were carrying load throughout the system, meaning the organization was managing its own ongoing structural fragility at the same time it was deploying capacity to help others. The system was functioning. It wasn't whole. Full restoration to pre-storm condition took months, for our system and for every utility the storm had touched. The storm passed in hours. The structural debt it created took far longer to retire.

None of that changes the governance argument.

We recovered not because the architecture held but because experienced people improvised intelligently under maximum compression. The neighboring systems that mobilized slower weren't less capable. They were in the same structural position, without the same combination of experienced judgment that happened to be present and functional in the right places at the right moment. That combination cannot be documented, institutionalized, or counted on to be present at the required level in every future event that demands it.

Intelligent improvisation under compression is not a governance strategy. It is what governance architecture is designed to make unnecessary.

The activation problem this event exposes is more demanding than it first appears. Activation thresholds built around damage confirmation are insufficient when stress arrives faster than confirmation is possible. Thresholds built around warning systems are insufficient when the event develops faster than warning infrastructure can track. Explosive cyclogenesis, by definition, outpaces both. The same structural condition appears elsewhere, in forms that look nothing like a utility storm. Financial contagion propagates across interconnected systems before detection is complete. Cyber events cascade through shared architecture faster than containment can be established. Supply chains fail simultaneously across concentrated upstream dependencies that nobody examined as a single point of vulnerability. The mechanism differs each time. The governance problem doesn't.

What pre-designed Emergency architecture provides isn't a guarantee of better outcomes. It is the removal of the hours consumed by constructing command structure under compression, hours that in any operational context carry direct human consequence. Every hour spent building what should have already existed is an hour of response that doesn't happen.

Pre-authorized thresholds must be tied to trajectory and development conditions, not solely to confirmed failure. The trigger for escalation cannot require certainty, because under compressed timelines, certainty arrives simultaneously with the closure of the window it was supposed to inform. Each escalation decision, from Primary to Alternate, through Contingency, down to Emergency posture, must be authorized before stress renders the authorization decision moot. It has to be defined during stability as a governance function, not negotiated in real time when compression has already consumed the time negotiation requires.

That is a governance decision. It cannot be delegated to the moment of stress, because the moment of stress is precisely when the cognitive conditions described earlier in this chapter are most fully in effect: time compressing, information degrading, the mind gravitating toward established narratives rather than structural reality.

The Southwest Georgia storm revealed what happens when activation architecture is absent. The Challenger decision reveals something different: what happens when the decision architecture is present but structurally incapable of holding a technical objection against organizational momentum.

What the record of the Challenger decision reveals is not a story about individual failure. It is a case study in what happens when an organization encounters a direct conflict between technical judgment and operational momentum, and has no decision architecture capable of resolving that conflict independently of the conditions producing it.

On the evening of January 27, 1986, engineers at Morton Thiokol presented a formal recommendation against launching the Space Shuttle Challenger the following morning. The concern, documented in the Presidential Commission report on the accident, centered on O-ring performance at low temperatures. The predicted launch temperature of 26 degrees Fahrenheit was far below the coldest previous launch, which had itself produced the most significant O-ring erosion in the program's history. The engineers could not prove with mathematical certainty that the shuttle would fail. What they could demonstrate was that the temperature range of the scheduled launch was outside the validated performance envelope of the joint seal system.

The recommendation not to launch was presented on a teleconference that included NASA program management. According to the Presidential Commission's findings and the firsthand account of Morton Thiokol engineer Roger Boisjoly, the recommendation was not received as a technical boundary. It was received as an obstacle to a schedule that carried significant programmatic and institutional weight. The burden of proof shifted in the room. The question was no longer whether it was safe to launch. It became whether the engineers could prove it was unsafe.

That shift is the cognitive and organizational condition this chapter has been describing. Under stable conditions, experienced people in that room had made sound decisions across years of successful missions. The performance record was real. The expertise was genuine. The commitment to the program and to the crew was without question. What arrived was not a failure of any of those qualities but a conflict between technical judgment and operational momentum that the decision architecture had no independent mechanism to resolve.

Morton Thiokol's management went offline from the teleconference to deliberate. According to Boisjoly's account, submitted to the Presidential Commission and available in the public record, the senior vice president turned to the supervising engineer and told him to take off his engineering hat and put on his management hat. The no-launch recommendation was reversed. The shuttle launched the following morning. Seventy-three seconds into flight, it was lost along with its crew.

The Presidential Commission's investigation concluded that the decision-making process itself was flawed, not the intentions of those within it. What it documented was an authority structure in which the channel for resolving technical objections ran upward through programmatic and institutional leadership rather than through an independent technical review process. When the engineering objection entered that channel at the level of pressure that existed that night, the channel was not designed to preserve the objection's weight against the organizational conditions surrounding it.

What the instruction to set aside the engineering judgment produced was not the compromise of one person's position. It collapsed the boundary between the technical layer and the management layer at the precise moment that boundary was the only remaining structural protection between the engineering objection and the launch decision. Two layers became one. The management layer, which should have functioned as an independent Alternate capable of reviewing the technical position and either confirming or escalating it, instead absorbed the organizational pressure and reversed the objection. The distinction between technical authority and management authority disappeared at the fracture point.

What remained above those collapsed layers offered no independent recourse. The authority structure that should have provided Contingency review was answerable to programmatic and institutional leadership, not to technical judgment. There was no Emergency tier that operated outside the pressure bearing down on the entire decision architecture simultaneously. Every layer that should have failed differently was instead failing the same way, in the same direction, toward the same outcome. The architecture had no depth at the moment it needed it most. When the boundary between the technical and management layers fell, there was nothing structurally independent left to hold.

A governance structure with pre-authorized conflict benchmarks would not have guaranteed a different outcome. It would have required that the engineering objection be examined through a pathway independent of the conditions that were absorbing it, before the decision could proceed. It would have redirected the decision-making process at the moment the conflict benchmark was met, rather than leaving the resolution of that conflict to an authority channel that was answerable to programmatic leadership rather than to technical judgment.

That is what the absence of a structural failsafe produces under duress. Not malice. Not negligence. Not a failure of the qualities that had made the people involved successful across years of demanding work. It produces the predictable outcome of a decision architecture that had no independent tier capable of holding a technical objection against organizational momentum when compression arrived and the established narrative exerted its pull.

The pattern did not begin with Challenger and did not end there. The National Commission investigating the Deepwater Horizon disaster concluded in its Chief Counsel's report that every technical failure traced back to an overarching failure of management, and its lead investigator found no instance where decision-makers had consciously chosen cost over safety. The architecture gave them no independent pathway to hold technical warnings against commercial and schedule pressure operating simultaneously. The Chernobyl disaster, examined extensively in Soviet and subsequent international investigations, revealed the same structural condition in a different system entirely: technical concerns present within an authority architecture that had no independent tier capable of holding them against institutional momentum. The decision to maintain speed through the North Atlantic ice field in April 1912, despite received warnings, demonstrated the same absence a century earlier and in the simplest possible form: no independent tier existed with the authority to hold the operational decision against the schedule pressure driving it.

The events differ across industries, cultures, and decades. The underlying architectural absence is the same.

The experience in southwest Georgia eventually produced this framework. But the framework exists because experience alone is not a plan. The conditions that made improvisation necessary that night were not the product of negligence. They were the product of planning built from prior storms, none of which had ever demanded what explosive cyclogenesis required.

Governance cannot anticipate every storm shape. It can require that activation thresholds be defined before the shape of the next one is known.

When the Primary fails, what survives next isn't determined by presumption, confidence, or assumption. It was determined long before the failure, by the governance decisions that either preserved structural independence or allowed it to erode, and by whether activation authority was defined in advance or left to be negotiated under compression.

Those two conditions are inseparable. Architecture without activation discipline is capability that cannot be deployed, present and functional but with no triggering mechanism when it is needed most.

CHAPTER 8

Architecture in Motion

There's a difference between understanding how architecture should work and seeing it work. The previous chapters established the framework, the diagnostic, and the governance responsibility. This chapter examines what happens when that discipline is actually applied, when leadership moves from structural awareness into structural interrogation of real decisions in real time.

That shift matters because it's where most governance efforts stall. Risk registers get updated. Dashboards get expanded. Framework language gets adopted. But the disciplined questioning that actually changes architectural outcomes, the kind that surfaces concentration before it hardens, that tests independence before stress reveals its absence, tends to remain episodic rather than embedded. This chapter is about what embedded looks like.

Every organization operates within a Primary architecture. Most can describe it in terms of output, efficiency, and reliability. Fewer can describe it in terms of structural dependency, and that gap is where exposure accumulates. The first step in putting architecture in motion isn't asset inventory. It's identifying enabling inputs: where throughput concentrates, which vendors cluster exposure, which geographic corridors carry disproportionate weight, which digital integrations centralize control, which authority pathways compress decision-making, and which capital channels underwrite continuity. That kind of examination can feel like looking for problems, but it's more accurately described as looking for facts that stability hasn't yet been forced to reveal.

Concentration isn't inherently flawed or discouraged. It's often efficient, sometimes necessary, and occasionally strategic. The issue isn't in the execution of concentration. It's in its invisibility. Every modernization effort, consolidation initiative, or integration decision shifts exposure somewhere. When those shifts aren't examined deliberately, independence compresses quietly while performance appears to strengthen.

Once the Primary is understood structurally, the conversation turns from catastrophe to something more common and more manageable: what happens if a central enabling input degrades? What happens if two degrade simultaneously? What happens if authority availability narrows while operational demand increases?

A centralized digital backbone may function flawlessly during isolated disruption. If the Alternate depends on that same backbone, redundancy exists but independence doesn't. Vendor ecosystems consolidated for efficiency may withstand localized interruption. Under upstream concentration, correlation emerges. Capital authorization that requires executive presence may function reliably during stability. Under synchronized stress, that pathway may narrow precisely when agility is required.

Redundancy adds margin within a pathway. Independence creates insulation between pathways. That distinction is architectural, and it's the difference between an organization that slows under stress and one that stops.

As stress intensifies, architecture descends through tolerance thresholds. Contingency posture isn't a diminished Primary. It's a simplified preservation of mission. Complex systems trend toward integration, and integration improves performance but increases coupling. Contingency deliberately reverses that density. It clarifies what must continue at all costs, which processes can degrade to manual execution, and which functions can pause without systemic harm. Emergency posture narrows further still. Authority concentrates. Communication simplifies. Capital activation becomes predefined rather than negotiated.

These tiers aren't theoretical constructs. They represent escalating tolerance architecture. If tiers inherit shared compression points, they share tolerance ceilings. Under cascading stress, they fail together. Putting architecture in motion means verifying that they don't.

Consider a multi-regional enterprise preparing to approve a major digital modernization initiative. The proposal is compelling. Data systems consolidate into a single integrated platform. Operational visibility centralizes. Vendor relationships streamline. Analytics strengthen. Cost savings are real. The roadmap is detailed. Cyber protections are described. The business case is sound.

The board begins where boards typically begin: financial return, vendor stability, regulatory alignment, operational efficiencies. Then a director asks a different question.

If this becomes our Primary operating architecture, what enabling inputs does it concentrate?

Management explains that consolidation improves transparency and reduces complexity. True. But concentration may also increase dependency. Does digital control now depend on a single cloud ecosystem? Do analytics rely on one upstream data pipeline? Does operational visibility flow through a unified backbone? Redundancy exists. Backups are mirrored. Recovery protocols are defined. But are those backups hosted within the same vendor environment? Do they rely on the same identity management architecture? Do they share geographic concentration?

The modernization proceeds. But it proceeds differently, with explicit examination of where concentration has increased, what Alternate architecture remains genuinely independent, and what Contingency posture simplifies intentionally if both Primary and Alternate are impaired.

Governance required that advancement be examined structurally before it hardened into exposure.

In another operational environment I worked in, a mission-critical supervisory control system had a newly constructed backup site to ensure operational redundancy. On paper, the configuration looked sound. Two sites, two control environments, documented fallback and rollover procedures. From a reliability standpoint, the investment was defensible, and the redundancy was real.

In practice, both sites sat in the same valley, and a review of historical storm damage confirmed that they shared the same vulnerability characteristic. The geographic decisions had been made during capital planning for the redundant site, based on operational proximity, which reduced costs and simplified both construction and operational logistics, all legitimate considerations. What wasn't examined was whether proximity also meant shared exposure, and whether the backup site could be affected by the same impacts as the primary site.

Under correlated disruption, a storm that compromises the primary site would also compromise the backup if identical conditions remained unaltered. And unlike a component failure that could be diagnosed and repaired sequentially, geographic coupling meant both sites would simultaneously face the same impairment at the moment restoration redundancy was needed.

The vulnerability wasn't created by incompetence. It emerged from unexamined geographic coupling that had not been evaluated as a governance question during planning and site selection. The capital allocation had been examined for cost, logistics, and operational benefit. It hadn't been examined for structural independence. The response didn't require abandoning the concept of a backup site or reversing the modernization, both judicious governance decisions. It required ensuring layered buffering through differentiation. What was needed was an insulated Contingency location capable of operating independently. This would preserve the modernization objectives while restoring the structural insulation the backup site had been presumed to provide.

The lesson isn't specific to supervisory control systems. Any capital decision that sites a backup or redundancy within the same hazard threshold as the primary, be it geographic, digital, logistical, or organizational, creates the same structural vulnerability. The redundancy appears complete on the balance sheet, but the coupled vulnerability isn't identified until stress reveals it.

Volatility exposes both differentiation and assumption, and it does so simultaneously across an entire competitive landscape. Organizations that compressed independence in pursuit of efficiency may have performed exceptionally during stability, but under synchronized stress they discover that options have narrowed and been systematically eliminated precisely when they matter most. Their management attention is consumed. Their capital is deployed defensively. Their strategic horizon contracts to the nearest crisis.

Institutions that differentiated their architecture experience the same external volatility from a structurally different position. They're managing disruption, not consumed by it. That difference in structural posture is what creates the capacity to act rather than react, to identify the openings volatility produces rather than simply trying to survive its effects. The flexibility to degrade intentionally without collapse, redeploy capability without negotiation delay, and capture opportunity while competitors focus on containment and reconfiguration decisions isn't a theoretical advantage. It's the practical consequence of architectural decisions made before volatility arrived to test them.

Under stress, structural independence without maneuverability becomes static, and maneuverability without structural independence becomes fragile. Governance discipline requires both to coexist, and that coexistence has to be designed before volatility tests whether it exists.

When PACE is embedded and rigorously applied, it does something that purely defensive resilience frameworks rarely accomplish: it preserves the structural conditions that allow leadership to function effectively under stress and move deliberately toward opportunity when volatility creates it. Failure remains not just possible but probable in any complex environment. Disruption will arrive. The question governance must answer in advance is whether the organization will be consuming its resilience when it does, or deploying it. That answer is architectural, and it has to be decided before volatility makes the question urgent.

CHAPTER 9

The Architecture of Differentiation

How Systems Fail Differently by Design

Most organizations believe they've achieved differentiation, and that belief is precisely the problem. They point to mirrored servers, backup generators, secondary vendors, documented succession plans, alternate facilities, and contingency binders. On paper, redundancy appears abundant and sufficient. Under correlated stress, they often discover that these protective, redundant layers compress together. What appeared diversified and independent proves structurally similar and functionally coupled.

Redundancy increases capacity within a pathway by providing more of the same and creating margin against isolated failure. Differentiation creates insulation between pathways, ensuring that when one system fails, another survives because it's built on materially distinct enabling inputs. The first improves performance within a tier. The second determines whether failure stays within one or propagates across several. That difference determines whether disruption is contained or cascades, and it's a governance responsibility, not an engineering preference.

Every operational layer rests on enabling inputs. Energy feeds production, digital control systems regulate flow, and data pathways route information. Vendors supply components, geographic corridors move people and goods, authority structures guide decisions, and capital channels sustain continuity. These inputs are taken for granted during stable conditions because they function reliably. Resilience evaluation typically begins at the output level, examining production capacity, uptime percentages, recovery time objectives, and replacement inventories. Those measures confirm operational readiness. They don't reveal structural independence.

Architectural differentiation starts with a different question: not just "do we have backup?" but "what does this depend upon?" That shift moves evaluation from visible redundancy to underlying dependency, and the difference between those two questions is where most governance examinations stop too soon.

An Alternate system that depends on the same digital backbone as the Primary may function during isolated disruption but will compress under correlated impairment, if the stressor that disabled the Primary travels the same pathway to the Alternate. A secondary vendor that sources from the same upstream manufacturer provides parallel capacity, not independence. A recovery site within the same hazard footprint may reduce travel time, but it doesn't fail differently, and failing differently is the only thing that matters under synchronized stress.

In practical terms, differentiation requires insulation across at least one enabling dimension that varies materially from the Primary. True differentiation requires that at least one critical enabling input vary materially from the Primary architecture. It doesn't require duplication across every dimension. It requires insulation at a decisive point.

Consider how concentration accumulates in practice. A financial institution centralizes its data recovery environment to a single geographic region to reduce operational complexity. A sound decision on its own terms. But if primary operations, backup systems, and recovery architecture all share the same regional infrastructure, the organization has reduced cost and complexity while creating a single class of stress capable of impairing all three simultaneously. The decisions weren't made recklessly, but concentration emerged from a series of individual, unvalidated rational ones, which is precisely why governance must examine the cumulative architectural effect rather than relying on the soundness of individual decisions.

Coupling isn't inherently dangerous. In many environments it enhances performance and simplifies oversight. It becomes a liability when it's mistaken for resilience, when the organization presumes that connected systems are also independent ones. Once concentration is visible, differentiation becomes a design decision rather than an accident, and that's where governance earns its weight.

At the governance level, differentiation isn't an operational preference. It's a fiduciary obligation. Boards are responsible not merely for performance continuity but for structural independence sufficient to prevent cascading impairment across critical tiers. When performance strength quietly converts into structural fragility through accumulated concentration, that conversion is a governance failure, not an operational one.

That insulation takes different forms depending on where concentration has accumulated. Geographic separation keeps critical assets outside shared hazard zones. Vendor diversification maintains upstream independence through suppliers that don't share manufacturing regions or logistics corridors. Digital segmentation ensures that a compromise of one control layer doesn't automatically propagate to the next. Distributed authority thresholds prevent decision-making from compressing into a single node under stress. Preconfigured capital triggers preserve financial activation pathways that operate independently of operational impairment. The form varies by context, domain, and need. The requirement doesn't.

Differentiation must also be validated before it can be trusted. Validation doesn't require theatrical crisis rehearsals. It requires disciplined reasoning applied calmly: if this layer fails, does that layer automatically compress? If this vendor is unavailable, does the entire supply chain stall? If this digital backbone is impaired, can simplified physical processes sustain core mission? If executive availability narrows under synchronized stress, does authority diffuse or concentrate?

These are architectural confirmations. Tactical drills test response. Structural reasoning confirms whether independence actually exists. When leaders can articulate clearly how independence is preserved, not rhetorically but structurally, confidence becomes grounded in design rather than assumption.

Architecture isn't static, and neither is differentiation. As vendors merge, infrastructure integrates, platforms centralize, and geographic footprints expand, independence erodes quietly. Authority pathways streamline in pursuit of efficiency, and performance dashboards rarely reveal that erosion until stress tests the system, which is precisely the moment when nothing can be done about it.

Differentiation that isn't periodically revalidated will erode. Consolidation is the natural drift of complex systems. Governance must actively counterbalance that drift through recurring structural review, not as a compliance exercise but as a standing discipline applied before stress makes the absence of it consequential.

Designing systems to fail differently is mature governance, not pessimism. It acknowledges that complexity increases vulnerability unless insulation is deliberately engineered and periodically confirmed. Failure remains possible in any complex environment. What governance determines is whether failure cascades or remains contained, and containment is what makes recovery possible.

Supply chain architecture deserves specific attention in this context. Supply chains are not linear procurement channels. They are the hidden dependency architecture behind operational continuity, and when that architecture is concentrated, opaque, or digitally exposed, a single disruption can disable functions far beyond the original point of failure.

Most organizations manage supply chain risk as a procurement or logistics function. Vendor relationships are tracked, contracts are maintained, and backup suppliers are identified. That is necessary. It is not sufficient. The governance question is structural: do the backup suppliers draw from the same upstream sources? Do they depend on the same transportation corridors, the same port infrastructure, the same digital platforms, or the same energy inputs as the primary? If they do, the supply chain has redundancy but not independence, and redundancy without independence is delay, not insulation.

The problem extends further than direct vendor relationships. Fourth-party risk, the suppliers of suppliers, the vendors of vendors, the digital platforms and logistics corridors that underlie multiple tiers of a supply chain without any single participant knowing it, is where modern supply chain concentration most dangerously accumulates. A software provider, a semiconductor fabricator, a port facility, or a cloud platform can sit three levels deep in multiple supply chains simultaneously, invisible to every organization depending on it, until the moment it fails. At that point, organizations that believed their supply chains were diversified discover they were drawing from the same hidden source. It is not governance's role to map every upstream dependency. It is governance's obligation to ensure that the oversight structures, integration platforms, and reporting mechanisms capable of surfacing that visibility exist at the operational level, and that their findings reach the governance layer before concentration hardens into unexamined exposure.

Applying PACE to supply chain architecture asks the same questions it asks everywhere else. What is the Primary supply pathway and what does it depend on? Does the Alternate fail differently, or does it share the same upstream concentration? What Contingency simplifies the supply requirement to its essential core if both are impaired? What Emergency authority exists to source outside normal channels, commit capital rapidly, and sustain core operations while the supply architecture is restored? These are not questions for procurement to answer in isolation. They are questions governance must require be answered, at the board and executive level, before consolidation decisions are approved, before vendor relationships are restructured, and before strategic sourcing initiatives are finalized. The structural examination belongs to governance. The operational detail belongs to the teams who execute it.

Cybersecurity infrastructure warrants the same structural examination applied to every other enabling input. Firewalls, identity management systems, endpoint protection platforms, and security operations functions are typically treated as protective layers that sit above the systems they defend. When those protective layers share the same digital backbone, the same vendor platform, or the same geographic concentration as the systems they are designed to protect, a compromise of the security infrastructure itself disables the protective function at the moment of maximum need. The organization loses not only a system but the governance layer designed to defend it. This is a concentration point of a particular kind: one whose failure is most consequential precisely because it was designed to prevent failure. Governance must require that cybersecurity architecture be examined for structural independence with the same discipline applied to every other enabling input.

Information integrity deserves specific attention within this context. A well-differentiated architecture can still be paralyzed if the decision-makers depending on it are receiving false information about which tiers are actually viable. Deliberate disinformation, manufactured reports of outages, manipulated sensor data, false signals about service availability or threat level, is a structural attack on the governance layer itself. It doesn't disable a system directly. It corrupts the inputs that determine how the architecture responds. The question governance must be able to answer is not only whether fallback tiers are structurally independent, but whether the information channels that activate and coordinate those tiers are themselves insulated from manipulation. An organization whose architecture is sound but whose decision inputs have been deliberately corrupted is functionally impaired.

When the Primary exceeds its tolerance threshold, what survives next? And is it structurally independent enough to endure the next level of compression? Those aren't rhetorical questions. Governance must be able to answer them before stress makes them urgent. But answering them is only the beginning. Structural discipline that preserves survivability under stress also preserves something most governance discussions never examine: the freedom to advance when others cannot.

CHAPTER 10

Strategic Maneuverability

Architected Optionality and Enterprise Application

Most resilience discussions stop at continuity, restoration, and recovery. Those are necessary goals, but not the only ones needed. They don't go far enough. Institutions don't exist solely to survive disruption. They exist to serve stakeholders, compete in markets, and advance their missions, and the structural discipline that preserves survivability under stress is the same discipline that preserves the capacity to act decisively when conditions provide opportunity. Organizations with differentiated architecture don't just absorb volatility, they move deliberately within it, and that capacity is what separates institutions that emerge from disruption stronger from those that spend months catching up.

The difference between an institution that freezes under volatility and one that moves deliberately within it isn't confidence or leadership quality. It's architecture. Specifically, it's whether the architecture was designed with optionality in mind or whether optionality was assumed to exist and discovered to be absent at the moment it was needed.

Architected Optionality is the deliberate structural design of an institution's resources, authority pathways, and preconfigured capital provisions so it can pivot under stress or reposition amid volatility without triggering a cascade. Its purpose is survivability across escalating tolerance thresholds, and it's strategic maneuverability designed before it's needed rather than improvised after volatility makes the absence of it urgent.

Most organizations design assets for singular purpose, and under stable conditions that approach is rational. Under stable conditions, assets are designed for singular purpose: facilities to produce, teams to specialize, platforms to integrate, and capital to concentrate where returns are strongest. Specialization improves throughput and lowers cost. The governance question that rarely gets asked is whether those same assets can serve an Alternate role when disruption occurs or pivot to capture opportunity when conditions shift.

Without prior modeling, reallocation under stress creates unintended consequences because the resource was never segmented, insulated, or authorized for pivot use, and the architecture to activate latent capability simply doesn't exist when stress arrives, and by then it's too late to build it.

The 2025 automotive aluminum crisis illustrates Architected Optionality failing at industry scale. Leading automakers had spent years optimizing their supply chains around lightweight aluminum designs, consolidating procurement to maximize efficiency and negotiating leverage. The logic was sound. The concentration was unexamined.

When a catastrophic fire destroyed a single domestic facility that Logistics Viewpoints reported supplied approximately 40 percent of the industry's automotive aluminum sheet, the assumption of domestic supply chain resilience collapsed immediately. Alternative domestic mills couldn't absorb the capacity deficit. Automakers were forced to source emergency imports, triggering punitive tariff penalties that compounded the supply disruption with a cost shock. Production lines were cut and assembly plants idled across the industry. The impact fell hardest on manufacturers whose flagship products depended on aluminum-intensive designs, with one leading automaker seeing production cut by more than half and facing reported commodity cost increases exceeding one billion dollars within a single operating cycle.

The structural lesson wasn't that aluminum consolidation was wrong. It was that consolidation through a single facility, regardless of whether domestic or overseas, created a compression point that no individual manufacturer had examined as a governance question. Each company had optimized its supply chain rationally. Nobody had asked what happens if the primary source fails and the Alternate draws from the same constrained pool. By the time the compression point failed, the options available were all bad, and the decisions that would have preserved maneuverability had been made years earlier without examining their structural consequence.

The crisis also produced something that concentrated organizations rarely recognize in the moment they're most constrained: opportunity. While production lines were idled and procurement teams were scrambling to source emergency aluminum at punitive tariff rates, a small number of manufacturers who had maintained diversified upstream supply relationships and multi-source procurement architectures found themselves in a structurally different position. They weren't immune to the disruption. But their architecture gave them options when the concentrated manufacturers had none. Some accelerated deliveries to capture market share from competitors who couldn't fulfill orders. Others secured longer-term supply agreements at favorable terms while constrained competitors were focused entirely on containment. The differentiation that had appeared inefficient during stability, the redundant supplier relationships, the diversified sourcing corridors, the slightly higher procurement costs, became a competitive asset the moment stress synchronized across the industry. That's not a theoretical benefit of structural discipline. It's what Architected Optionality actually produces when volatility arrives.

The same applies to teams. A highly specialized operations team serves as Primary execution during stability. Under synchronized disruption, that team could be redeployed to reinforce restoration, stabilize infrastructure, or mitigate cascading strain. Under volatile market conditions, the same team might pivot toward emerging opportunity if insulated from the stress affecting the Primary revenue channel. But that flexibility doesn't materialize without prior modeling, authorization, and structural protection from the same constraints that impair the Primary.

When leadership maps tiers deliberately through PACE, they begin to see where resources serve cross purposes. A production asset that can double as a Contingency stabilizer, a digital platform that will also provide a segmented recovery channel, a logistics network that pivots to support alternate distribution, and a field team that transitions to a rapid response unit when needed. The problem is that none of these roles materialize without prior structural design. Those capabilities may exist, but the capacity to act on them has to be developed in advance.

Recognizing that these options exist matters far less than structuring them, and structuring them is governance. When the same enabling inputs power both Primary and Alternate roles, pivoting becomes illusion rather than option. Unclear authorization thresholds delay redeployment, and capacity optimized to the point where no reserve margin exists eliminates maneuverability precisely when it's most needed.

Capital allocation decisions should not only ask what an asset produces under stability but what alternate role it can fulfill under volatility. Team structures and digital integration decisions warrant the same examination. Can the team pivot if the Primary revenue channel is impaired? Can the digital architecture segment if the integrated platform fails? Those are governance questions, not operational ones. The objective is structural flexibility that performs under conditions the Primary architecture can't sustain. Redundancy alone doesn't get you there.

Organizations that apply PACE rigorously no longer view resources as fixed production units; instead, they see them as nodes within a reconfigurable survivability architecture that can be redeployed or repurposed when conditions require it.

Winston Churchill's observation that a good crisis should never go to waste wasn't strategic opportunism. It was structural realism. Organizations that retain the architecture to act when others are constrained don't manufacture opportunity from disruption. They simply remain capable of recognizing and pursuing it when it appears, because their structure hasn't been consumed by the disruption itself.

Resilience and growth intersect precisely here, and it's worth being specific about what that intersection actually looks like in practice. When volatility synchronizes across an industry or a market, it doesn't affect all participants equally. It affects them in proportion to their structural concentration. Organizations whose architecture is tightly coupled compress together. Their management teams focus on containment, their capital is consumed by emergency response, and their strategic capacity narrows to a single question: how do we survive this? Organizations whose architecture has been deliberately differentiated face the same external conditions but from a structurally different position. Their fallback tiers are holding. Their capital is not being consumed by crisis response at the same rate. Their leadership has predefined thresholds rather than improvised decisions. That structural difference is what creates the opening.

The opening isn't always obvious. It may be a market share opportunity created by a competitor's production shutdown. It may be a talent acquisition opportunity created by a competitor's workforce reduction. It may be a customer relationship opportunity created by a competitor's delivery failure. It may be a strategic partnership opportunity created by a competitor's capital constraint. The form varies but the structural condition that makes it accessible remains the same. Organizations with differentiated architecture can move toward those openings because their architecture can support movement. Organizations without it are too consumed by containment to see them, let alone act on them.

That's what Architected Optionality ultimately provides. Not just survivability. The structural confidence to advance when others are retreating.

Two sets of governance questions follow from this. The first addresses stress: if an asset serves as Primary production, what Alternate role can it fulfill under disruption? What enabling inputs must be insulated to allow pivot? What authority permits rapid redeployment? What capacity margin preserves maneuverability when the Primary is impaired?

The second addresses opportunity: if a competitor's architecture fails under synchronized stress, which of our assets are positioned to serve their customers, capture their market share, or fill their supply gap? What structural conditions would need to be in place for us to move toward that opening rather than away from it? What would prevent us from acting, and is that constraint architectural or operational?

The organization that can answer both has built something more than defensive resilience. It has built the structural confidence to advance when others are retreating.

CHAPTER 11

Applied Structural Analysis

When Architecture Is Tested by Correlated Stress

The examples in this chapter come from operational environments examined directly over the course of this work. They aren't presented as disaster narratives. They're structural examinations, and the lessons they carry aren't specific to utilities or storms. They appear wherever systems depend on layered inputs and wherever the planning model hasn't been tested against simultaneous external degradation.

Large-scale events strip away the illusion of isolation. When stress spreads across geography, supply chains, workforce availability, communications networks, and infrastructure simultaneously, hidden dependencies surface. What seemed improbable becomes reality, what appeared separate is revealed to be connected, and what was assumed to be backup reveals its parallel exposure.

Regional Compression Under Correlated Stress

The 1993 Storm of the Century wasn't merely a weather event. It was a synchronized systems event that stretched from Central America to Canada and impacted more than half the US population. Transmission and distribution lines were damaged across the entire affected region, transportation corridors were restricted, material supply slowed, field crews worked under hazardous conditions, public expectations intensified, and information channels became saturated simultaneously.

The storm didn't test effort. It tested structure.

For utilities across the affected region, the Primary operating architecture had performed reliably for decades. Restoration plans were practiced. Mutual aid agreements were active. Leadership experience reinforced confidence that recovery, though difficult, would follow familiar patterns. Under isolated impairment, that confidence was justified. This event was not isolated impairment.

Pressure arrived across domains at the same time. Workforce, materials, transportation, communications, and energy supply were all affected concurrently. What would have been manageable in sequence became genuinely difficult in parallel, and difficult in parallel spirals into unmanageability under compressing decision velocity.

This is tier compression in practice. It occurs when stress exceeds the separation between tiers, and instead of strain being absorbed progressively, Primary first, then Alternate, then Contingency, pressure reaches multiple layers at once because those layers share common foundations.

In regional compression, geographically correlated disruption narrows the separation between tiers. Redundancy may activate, but insulation weakens. Alternate pathways draw from the same workforce pools. Mutual aid depends on regions that are equally affected. Transportation routes that normally provide flexibility are impaired simultaneously. Supplier networks slow everywhere at once.

Communication systems that can manage localized surge struggle under sustained, multi-domain demand.

Under these conditions, the time between escalation decisions shrinks. Decision-makers are forced to act while visibility is incomplete. What was designed as layered protection begins to behave as a unified system under strain.

The practical question is direct: if the Primary fails under this kind of pressure, do the Alternate and Contingency fail for the same reason? If they do, separation is thinner than assumed.

Primary was built for stability, and it performed as designed. Restoration procedures assumed localized disruption, redundancy allowed rerouting, workforce mobilization assumed staggered impact, and communication systems were designed to handle surge rather than simultaneous saturation across multiple regions. The design was sound for the conditions it was built to handle. It wasn't built for this.

Alternate strategies existed. Neighboring utilities, contractors, mutual aid networks, and supplier agreements provided additional capacity for larger events. On paper, this appeared resilient. In practice, many of these alternate pathways relied on the same upstream conditions as the Primary. Mutual aid depended on utilities that were themselves under strain. Transportation routes were impaired across entire corridors. Suppliers were facing identical material shortages. Digital communication systems were processing demand from every affected region simultaneously.

Redundancy existed but separation was limited, and as the storm expanded, alternate capacity encountered the same constraints affecting the Primary. What was designed as backup began to operate under the same constraints. The impairment was no longer isolated. It was shared.

Shared impairment means shared dependency. Shared dependency means insufficient structural independence between tiers. That condition is architectural. The storm didn't create it. It revealed it.

Contingency planning had not been deeply institutionalized beyond restoration to full capacity. Structured degradation, identifying which functions must continue and which could pause temporarily, had not been operationalized at scale. Under extended pressure, restoration speed was no longer the only concern. Preservation of core mission became central. That shift had not been formally embedded in architecture.

Emergency posture assumes that reinforcement may not arrive, or may arrive too late. It assumes that upstream system impairment is not only possible but likely under simultaneous stress. That level of independence had not been seriously modeled. The storm didn't create fragility. It revealed compression that had accumulated quietly through years of planning built around assumptions that had never been tested against simultaneous external degradation.

Operational teams execute within the architecture they inherit. When compression narrows tiers simultaneously, it isn't a failure of effort. It reflects prior structural decisions and the cumulative erosion produced by unrevealed degradation, tolerated inefficiencies, deferred insulation, and confirmation bias built on a performance record that stability had never challenged.

Structural Concentration in a Two-Source System

During the same storm, a small rural utility faced a different but equally instructive challenge. Its largest customer, a high-load agricultural operation, depended on continuous power during extreme temperature conditions. Loss of service wasn't inconvenient. It threatened survival.

The utility supplied the facility through two distribution feeds, each sourced from separate substations with different upstream transmission lines. On paper, the design appeared sound, with two feeds sourced from separate substations with different upstream transmission lines. Each feed had been designed to sustain the load if the other failed, single-line disruption had been modeled, and load transfer procedures were in place.

What had not been modeled was the simultaneous disruption of both supply paths, and specifically the fact that both distribution feeders ultimately attached to the same two poles near the customer's property.

Under storm conditions, upstream transmission and substation supply were affected. Restoration efforts appropriately prioritized bulk supply, and one transmission line and substation were restored in time to begin stabilizing conditions. But the most significant constraint didn't originate upstream. It originated at the convergence point.

The two shared poles, critical to both distribution supply sources, were compromised. At the transmission level, independence appeared intact. At the distribution level convergence point, it was not. Redundancy was visible in the diagrams. Dependency was hidden in physical convergence.

On-site generation was limited and not designed to sustain full operational load. Utility restoration resources were already stretched by regional conditions. Workforce, materials, and prioritization decisions were under pressure simultaneously. Without prior recognition of the mutual compression at the point of concentration, the vulnerability only became visible under collapse.

Primary assumed either feed could sustain the load. Modeling focused on single-point failure. Alternate was the second feed, which provided delay under isolated disruption. But because both feeds converged at the same poles, independence was incomplete. Contingency planning had not defined partial-load preservation strategies specific to this customer under dual-junction loss. Emergency architecture would have required true physical separation at the convergence point or substantial pre-integrated backup generation capable of sustaining critical operations for an extended period.

The utility didn't lack effort or commitment. It lacked insulation at the point of concentration. Two poles carried disproportionate structural consequence. Their simultaneous loss may have been unlikely, but it still happened.

Fragility concentrates at critical nodes, not through scale but through density, and density at a single convergence point can carry consequences far beyond what was imagined. Concentration at critical nodes is discoverable through disciplined structural review. When it remains hidden, it's typically because design interrogation stopped at visible redundancy rather than physical convergence.

Field personnel restore within the physical boundaries they are given. If convergence points concentrate consequence, that density wasn't created during crisis. It was embedded during design, approval, capital allocation, and systematic optimization. The storm revealed it. Governance created the conditions for it.

Sequential Tier Elimination Through Unexamined Capital Decisions

The two storm examples demonstrate structural failure under acute external stress. The pattern they reveal, redundancy without independence, appears in environments where the stress arrives slowly, through a sequence of governance decisions that each appeared sound in isolation and were never examined for their combined structural effect.

In 2000, Toys R Us faced a genuine strategic problem: building an independent digital channel from scratch was expensive, technically demanding, and uncertain in outcome. The company was the dominant specialty toy retailer in the United States, with a recognized brand and a physical retail footprint that had made it a category leader for decades. E-commerce was accelerating and the competitive pressure was real.

The decision to partner with Amazon addressed that problem directly. The partnership gave Toys R Us immediate e-commerce presence but eliminated its autonomous online presence entirely, redirecting customers who visited ToysRUs.com to Amazon instead. The decision was rational and the partnership performed well initially, appearing to solve the digital challenge efficiently.

What it eliminated, without being examined as an elimination, was the company's independent digital channel. The Alternate pathway that a future under intensifying competitive pressure would require had been transferred to a counterparty whose interests would eventually diverge. When Amazon subsequently allowed competing toy sellers onto its platform, Toys R Us had no independent online presence to fall back on. The Alternate had been handed away in the transaction that appeared to create it.

The 2005 leveraged buyout compounded the structural condition. According to the company's own public filings, the acquisition placed more than five billion dollars in debt on the company's balance sheet, consuming capital that would otherwise have been available for competitive response. The capital that would have been required to build an independent digital channel, modernize the physical retail experience, and fund competitive response was precommitted to lenders. The company was operationally profitable on an earnings basis. It was structurally incapable of funding the adaptation its competitive environment required.

Neither decision was made carelessly. The Amazon partnership was a considered response to a real competitive threat. The capital structure reflected the financing conventions of its era. Both decisions were evaluated on the terms that governance normally applies:

strategic fit, financial return, competitive positioning, and operational feasibility. On those terms, both were defensible.

What neither decision received was a structural lens examining what the other was simultaneously removing. That lens didn't exist in the evaluation process, not because governance was negligent, but because the question of tier independence wasn't part of the standard framework through which major strategic and capital decisions were reviewed. The partnership eliminated digital independence. The debt structure eliminated capital flexibility. Neither elimination was visible as an elimination at the time it occurred. Together they produced an organization whose Primary retail channel was under sustained competitive siege, whose Alternate digital channel had been transferred to a counterparty with competing interests, and whose capital position made constructing a genuine replacement structurally impossible.

A PACE examination would have surfaced this condition before either decision was finalized. Not as a prediction of failure, not as a critique of the decisions themselves, but as a question the evaluation process should have included: if the Primary retail channel comes under sustained pressure, what is the Alternate that fails differently? If the Alternate depends on a counterparty whose interests may diverge, what is the Contingency that preserves independent market access? If both are compromised, what capital flexibility exists to construct Emergency architecture?

Those questions, present in the evaluation process before either decision was finalized, would have made the combined structural consequence visible. Their absence wasn't a failure of intent. It was a gap in the analytical framework that governed how major decisions were examined. The decisions accumulated. The architecture that resulted had no independent tier capable of sustaining the organization when its Primary channel came under the pressure that its competitive environment was already generating.

The financial collapse that followed was the visible consequence of structural concentration that had developed incrementally through individually sound decisions, none of which had been examined against what the previous one had already removed from the architecture. That is not a governance failure in the conventional sense. It is what happens when the structural lens is missing from the evaluation process entirely.

Well-considered decisions will sometimes backfire, smart strategic moves will sometimes fail, and unexpected obstacles and crises will materialize that no planning model anticipated. That is not a failure of leadership or judgment. It is the operating condition that every institution navigates. What PACE provides is not a guarantee against those outcomes. It provides two things that standard evaluation frameworks don't. It makes the combined structural consequence of sequential decisions visible before they accumulate into exposure that cannot be reversed. And it builds the independent tier architecture that gives the organization genuine options when a decision does backfire, when the unexpected obstacle arrives, or when the emergency materializes that nobody modeled. The question isn't whether decisions will be imperfect. It is whether the architecture they produce preserves the independence to respond when reality diverges from the plan.

Regional compression, structural concentration at a physical node, and sequential tier elimination through capital decisions are three different failure patterns. The stress mechanisms differ, the sectors differ, and the timelines differ, but what they share is the same underlying condition. In each case, the redundancy appeared independent and wasn't, and the examination came only after stress had already determined the outcome.

The pattern is not sector-specific. It is architectural. And architecture is determined by governance decisions made long before the stress arrives.

CHAPTER 12

Structural Accountability

Leadership Under Compression

When systems compress, the question that matters isn't who performed well in the moment. It's who owned the architecture before compression began.

Crisis management governs performance during compression. Structural accountability governs the architecture that determined how much compression the organization could absorb before options ran out.

Operational leaders manage stress in real time. They stabilize systems, restore service, and protect people. That work is real and it's demanding, but it operates within the architectural boundaries that governance established, and when those boundaries are too narrow, operational execution cannot compensate for an architecture that was never designed to hold under synchronized stress.

Executive leadership shapes those boundaries. They determine whether redundancy is preserved or removed, whether Alternates are funded or deferred, whether escalation thresholds are explicit or assumed. Boards define exposure by determining whether independence is preserved or compressed as complexity increases. These are structural decisions, and they carry structural accountability.

Resilience is an intentional structural condition. Without deliberate engineering, structure drifts toward concentration over time. Under stability, drift is often rewarded because it improves performance. Other times it goes unnoticed, but the slow compression of independence always shadows its movement. The weakened structural state only surfaces under stress, when the structural decisions that were made, deferred, or avoided become visible and consequential.

As stress compounds and tolerance thresholds degrade, structural concentration that once appeared efficient buckles under load. Decision rights narrow, information routes converge, and capital flexibility tightens simultaneously. If optionality was not deliberately distributed in advance, the organization discovers the severity of its limits precisely when adaptation is most difficult, and when stress surfaces the accumulated concentration, the architectural decisions that created those limits are no longer reversible.

Focusing on crisis management after disruption begins is the natural, necessary response. It doesn't provide structural accountability. That accountability was either embedded in the architecture before disruption arrived or it wasn't, and by the time crisis management activates, the answer is already fixed.

Structural accountability must be named and owned explicitly. Whether embedded within risk oversight, audit structures, executive review, or board mandate, survivability cannot remain implied. It must be explicitly owned, because what isn't explicitly owned defaults to habit, tradition, or optimism, and none of those survive synchronized stress.

Fiduciary responsibility extends beyond financial performance to stewardship of structural independence. That stewardship requires explicit structural review, and the examination must be substantive enough to surface concentration before stress does. Tier independence, authority dispersion, capital activation thresholds, modernization exposure shifts, and points of structural concentration must be examined deliberately before stress makes the examination urgent and the findings actionable only in retrospect.

Under layered stress, three compressions occur simultaneously: information degrades, time contracts, and authority narrows. Ambiguous authority thresholds cause hesitation that compounds exposure. Partial succession clarity fragments decision authority at exactly the moment it needs to be unified. Complicated capital activation pathways evaporate precisely when flexibility is most needed.

Structural discipline requires sufficient clarity to act before tolerance thresholds are exceeded, not perfect information. Waiting for certainty under compound stress surrenders maneuverability. Acting with confident, disciplined sufficiency before certainty arrives is architectural preparation expressed through timely authority, and timely authority requires that thresholds be defined before compression makes definition impossible.

Budget authority concentrates. Vendor reliance concentrates. Technical expertise concentrates. Decision rights concentrate. Over time, what once appeared diversified can silently unify through modernization, integration, or consolidation. Structural accountability acknowledges that favorable conditions are not permanent conditions and demands that authority architecture, capital allocation, and tier independence be examined deliberately rather than assumed implicitly.

Crisis doesn't create fragility. It reveals whether fragility was embedded through architectural inattention. The structural conditions that determine outcomes under compression were established long before the compression began, through capital decisions, modernization priorities, deferred structural examinations, and untested assumptions.

Leadership under compression exposes whether resilience was deliberately engineered or quietly assumed. When it was engineered, compression confirms the architecture. When it wasn't, the problem isn't the compression itself. The problem is that the decisions capable of changing that outcome had to be made long before compression arrived, in capital reviews, modernization approvals, and governance conversations where structural independence was never on the agenda.

CHAPTER 13

Institutionalizing Structural Discipline

Most organizations respond effectively to disruption once. The response is disciplined, the communication is clear, and the recovery demonstrates genuine organizational capability. Afterward, reports get written, lessons get identified, and commitments get made. In the months that follow, structural discipline feels real because the memory of what happened is still fresh.

Then the operational tempo resumes. Budget priorities reassert themselves. Leadership attention returns to growth and performance. The lessons become narrative. The discipline becomes episodic. And the next disruption arrives into an organization that responded well once but never embedded what that response required.

Most organizations understand the need for structural discipline, at least in the aftermath of disruption. The harder question is whether they make the strategic, sometimes controversial, decision to build it into the systems, processes, and governance expectations that outlast individual memory and remain intact when stress arrives in forms the organization has yet to encounter.

At the governance level, the PACE Resilience Framework isn't activated during disruption. It's expressed through decisions made during stability. Without institutionalization, it becomes reactive rather than architectural, invoked when things go wrong rather than embedded in how decisions get made when things are going right.

The primary obstacle to institutionalization is incentive misalignment. Operational domains are rewarded for efficiency, integration, cost reduction, and scale. Finance consolidates and optimizes capital deployment. Procurement seeks leverage through vendor concentration. Digital leadership advances unified platforms to increase visibility and coordination. Strategy accelerates growth where advantage appears strongest. These incentives aren't wrong. They simply aren't aligned with preserving tier differentiation, and without governance intervention, optimization will dominate because optimization is what gets measured, rewarded, and celebrated.

Structural discipline operates on a different incentive track from performance optimization, and without a deliberate counterforce at the governance level, that separation widens quietly until stress reveals it.

When cross-domain initiatives continually exclude structural revalidation, the insulation between layers narrows. Modernization unifies enabling platforms across tiers, consolidation streamlines performance while quietly coupling what were once separate response mechanisms to shared infrastructure. Over time that coupling compresses independence without anyone having made a single decision to do so. Recognizing that this is structural pressure rather than failure of intent is important precisely because it identifies where the counterforce must be applied: not in correcting individual decisions but in changing the governance conditions that produce them.

Strategic initiatives reshape exposure whether examined or not. Geographic expansion can intensify regional compression while strengthening market position. Digital integration can increase efficiency by unifying enabling infrastructure across tiers while simultaneously eroding structural independence. Vendor consolidation may streamline costs but merge upstream logistics. Modernization initiatives that improve reliability can increase shared dependencies that narrow independence under stress. Without structural evaluation, decisions that appear beneficial in isolation can cumulatively compress architecture in ways that none of them would have individually.

Institutional discipline requires that major strategic initiatives be examined through an additional lens beyond financial projection and operational performance. Leadership must be able to articulate the structural consequence of a major proposal before approving it. How does it shift Primary architecture? Does a viable and funded Alternate still exist after it's implemented? How does it affect Contingency pathways, and where does Emergency reliance increase as a result? When applied consistently, PACE becomes a structural litmus test for advancement. It ensures that ambition doesn't silently erode independence across tiers and provides governance with defensible assurance that intended outcomes remain achievable under stress rather than compromised by unexamined concentration.

Capital decisions define what becomes Primary and what can realistically survive as Alternate or Contingency. Facilities, fleet investments, digital platforms, energy systems, cybersecurity infrastructure, data environments, and vendor ecosystems shape exposure for years, sometimes decades. Capital decisions are typically evaluated for return on investment, efficiency gains, and competitive advantage. Institutionalizing structural discipline requires an additional layer of examination: does this investment increase concentration in a critical domain, remove structural insulation that previously preserved survivability, or narrow tier independence as integration expands?

Not all redundancy is waste. Some of it is structural insulation, and the distinction between the two has to be visible at the governance level before redundancy removal decisions are made. When redundancy is removed solely to streamline operations without examining tier differentiation, survivability pathways narrow unintentionally. What appears efficient in one budget cycle may reveal structural rigidity under compression. PACE reframes redundancy not as waste or virtue but as architecture. It evaluates consequence and preserves independence without defending inefficiency.

Procurement practices illustrate how concentration accumulates without anyone intending it. Vendor diversification can appear distributed while remaining structurally unified through shared upstream dependencies. Two vendors may appear distinct while drawing from the same upstream manufacturer, sharing logistics corridors, running on the same digital backbone, or depending on the same energy source. On paper, exposure appears distributed. Under correlated disruption, dependency reveals itself as unified. Institutional discipline requires procurement evaluation that extends beyond direct contracts to examine shared upstream dependencies across manufacturers, infrastructure corridors, digital platforms, energy sources, and logistics pathways.

Executive dashboards are designed to track performance. They track uptime, service continuity, financial stability, and compliance adherence. Reliability can coexist with increasing structural coupling, and those dashboards won't reveal that. Structural discipline requires reporting that surfaces concentration mapping, tier validation, and authority threshold clarity alongside performance metrics. These elements should carry the same governance weight as financial exposure because survivability is a fiduciary condition, not an operational preference.

Governance review should deliberately examine where structural coupling has increased, where tier independence has narrowed, where modernization has shifted exposure, and where redundancy has been removed. Without periodic revalidation, institutions drift incrementally. Vendors consolidate, platforms integrate, geographic exposure shifts, and authority lines compress without any single decision crossing the threshold that would trigger governance review. Each adjustment may be rational individually. Collectively they produce structural density that only becomes visible under synchronized disruption.

What revalidation actually looks like in practice is worth examining, because the term is easy to endorse in principle and rarely defined in operational terms. Two cases from operational environments illustrate both what the examination produces and what consistently prevents it from happening as a standing discipline rather than a crisis response.

In the Solomon Islands, a development agency operating an economic advancement project on Guadalcanal and the adjacent islands found itself in a deteriorating security environment. Smoldering internal conflict was intensifying, and the question of expatriate exfiltration became urgent enough to demand a formal examination of what the architecture actually looked like.

What the examination found was a plan with apparent redundancy that had no structural independence. Multiple exfiltration routes existed on paper. Different roads, different approaches, different starting points across the island. The planning had been done. The options had been documented. What nobody had examined was where those routes converged. Every one of them fed into the same half mile of road through the same intersections before reaching the airport terminal. The airport itself was the only viable Primary. It was not directly targeted in the conflict, but it sat adjacent to the city center, and any demonstration or civil action in the urban area affected access to it as collateral consequence. The threat wasn't to the airport. It was to the conditions that made it reachable.

The redundancy in the existing plan was different routes to the same compression point, under the same exposure, at the moment the exfiltration requirement would be triggered. That's not redundancy. It's the same plan with different starting lines.

The examination produced a genuinely redesigned architecture. A viable Alternate was established that routed around the urban dependency. A Contingency was developed that was harder to execute but preserved the option when both Primary and Alternate were compromised. An Emergency exfiltration plan was put in place that was stripped to its essentials, low-dependency, and operable under the most degraded conditions the environment could produce. The tiers were differentiated. Each failed differently from the one above it. The architecture that resulted from the examination bore little resemblance to what had existed before it.

None of that examination happened as a standing governance discipline. It happened because the security environment deteriorated to the point where deferral was no longer possible. The examination produced sound architecture. The trigger was external pressure, not institutional practice.

The second case is structurally different in scale and consequence but identical in its governance lesson. In East Africa, an assessment examined market access for smallholder farmers attempting to move from subsistence to market-oriented agriculture. The existing architecture had three apparent options. Buyers came to the village and purchased crops for resale in town. When buyers weren't available or prices were unacceptable, farmers could hire transport to reach market directly. When transport was too costly, manual movement by hand or animal cart served as the fallback.

The examination revealed that these weren't three independent options. They were three expressions of the same structural condition. The buyers controlled the Primary, set the price, and had every incentive to suppress it. Hired transport was available but charged fees that eliminated the margin that reaching market was supposed to provide. Manual transport was physically limited to quantities that made market access impractical for anything beyond the most local exchange. Most critically, all three options shared the same fundamental exposure: the farmers had no storage capacity, no pricing information, and no negotiating leverage in any tier of the architecture. They could not hold crops when prices were low, they could not know what prices actually were, and they could not credibly use one channel as a threat against another because all of them led to the same outcome: sell at whatever terms were offered, or don't sell at all.

The compression point wasn't a road or an intersection. It was the total absence of structural independence across every apparent option simultaneously.

The assessment produced an architecture that addressed the shared exposure at each tier. A consolidated transport arrangement created genuine Primary access to market on terms the farmers didn't have to accept from buyers. Temporary storage capacity gave farmers an Alternate that allowed them to wait out periods when transport was unavailable or prices were unfavorable, breaking the forced-sale dynamic that buyers depended on. A satellite phone service at a central location provided real-time market pricing, destroying the information asymmetry that had been the buyers' primary source of leverage across every tier of the existing architecture.

The satellite phone is worth noting specifically. It was low-tech, low-cost, and independent of the road infrastructure that constrained every other element of the architecture. When transport was unavailable and storage was exhausted, the ability to know the actual market price and negotiate from that knowledge was the one tool that shared none of the enabling constraints of the tiers above it. That's Emergency architecture in its most practical form: simple, durable, and genuinely independent.

Both cases produced sound architecture. Neither examination was triggered by a standing governance discipline. One was triggered by a deteriorating security environment. The other by an external assessment mandate. In both cases, what the examination found was an architecture that had apparent options and no structural independence. In both cases, the result was a genuinely redesigned set of tiers that failed differently from one another.

Both cases demonstrate that revalidation produces significant value, with tangible and intangible returns that the numbers that follow confirm.

Structural examination has a real price. It is not the price of a training exercise, a tabletop scenario, or a generic risk assessment. It is the price of determining whether the organization's fallback options are genuinely independent, which requires examining the actual dependencies behind each tier, not the documented assumptions about them. That work takes time, requires access, and produces findings that are sometimes unwelcome. It costs money.

Every organization pays for structural resilience one way or another. Intentionally, before stress arrives, through examination and deliberate architecture. Or involuntarily, during failure, at dramatically higher cost through unnegotiated emergency procurement, extended restoration timelines, improvised command structures, and deferred repairs carrying load for months. The regulatory and reputational exposure that follows a failure governance cannot demonstrate it examined in advance compounds all of it.

The Solomon Islands exfiltration architecture review described in this chapter cost approximately $27,000 in professional fees plus expenses. That engagement examined a plan with apparent redundancy, identified the compression point where every route converged on the same half mile of road, and produced a redesigned architecture with genuinely differentiated tiers. The development agency left that engagement with an exfiltration plan that would function under the conditions that would actually trigger it. Arranging emergency alternate exfiltration for eight staff members during an active crisis was estimated at more than $250,000 in direct costs alone, based on discussions with regional providers capable of executing that operation. An active emergency response, with security coordination, crisis management, potential project termination, and the exposure that follows a failure governance could not demonstrate it had examined, would have been many times that figure. The examination cost $27,000. The alternative cost structure starts at a quarter of a million and compounds from there.

That is the economic argument for structural discipline stated plainly. The examination is not cheap. The alternative is more expensive, and it arrives when the organization has the least capacity to manage it.

What governance must require is that this comparison be made before stress forces it, not after.

Authority thresholds must be defined before compression occurs, not negotiated while it is underway. They should not be improvised during volatility. They must be architected during stability and reviewed as structure evolves. Clear thresholds reduce cognitive load under stress, preserve decision velocity, and prevent negotiation over authority while time compresses. Governance maturity is measured by the clarity embedded before disruption occurs, not by the speed of response after it begins.

The absence of structural discipline produces shallow resilience and reactive response. Disruption prompts temporary correction, lessons are discussed but not embedded, and architecture remains unchanged until the next event forces the conversation again. Where discipline exists procedurally but not architecturally, plans are written, exercises are conducted, and preparedness is assumed, yet capital decisions, procurement practices, and strategic initiatives proceed without consistent interrogation of tier independence and correlation exposure.

Genuinely embedded discipline ensures capital allocation, procurement, reporting structures, authority thresholds, and strategic initiatives are all routinely evaluated through structural differentiation, and exposure shifts are examined before they accumulate rather than after they cascade.

Institutions that embed structural discipline don't eliminate disruption, but they prevent systemic failure cascade. Failure gets contained, recoverability is preserved, and maneuverability survives the stress that would otherwise consume it.

Structural discipline that is genuinely embedded shapes how proposals are evaluated, how capital is approved, how procurement is structured, and how reporting is framed. It becomes habit rather than initiative, and that's the only form of structural discipline that actually persists.

CHAPTER 14

The Executive Decision Audit

Institutions rarely fail because leaders lacked intelligence or good judgment. They falter because the structural implications of decisions weren't examined before momentum made examination uncomfortable and reversal impractical.

Every material decision accumulates architecture. Capital investments, vendor consolidations, digital integrations, financing structures, geographic expansions, and governance adjustments all reshape structural exposure in ways that extend well beyond their immediate objectives. Most of those decisions are rational, many are beneficial, and some are genuinely necessary. But each carries structural consequence that performance projections and financial models don't capture, and that consequence compounds quietly until stress reveals it.

The Executive Decision Audit is the governance instrument designed to examine that structural consequence before decisions harden into exposure that can no longer be corrected without significant cost or disruption.

It's a governance instrument applied at the moment of decision, distinct from forensic review, compliance documentation, and risk management in a specific and important way. Enterprise Risk Management identifies, categorizes, and tracks exposure across operational, financial, regulatory, and strategic domains. That function remains essential. The Executive Decision Audit does something different. ERM evaluates risk categories in isolation. The audit evaluates how a decision may unify otherwise separate risks through shared architecture that wasn't visible when each risk was examined independently. That's a different analytical layer, and it's the one that matters most when concentration is the problem.

What risk literature describes as convergence is architectural concentration revealed under stress. Structural coupling is what creates fragility, and the audit is designed to surface that coupling before a decision is approved rather than after disruption makes it consequential.

Governance applies the audit when structural conditions shift, specifically when a material decision is about to alter the architecture the organization depends on. The audit earns its place at structural inflection points. These include capital investments that reshape infrastructure, vendor consolidations that concentrate upstream reliance, digital integrations that unify enabling platforms across tiers, and governance adjustments that redefine authority thresholds. Geographic expansions, financing restructuring, and any initiative that materially shifts how the organization depends on shared inputs all qualify.

Material initiatives often emerge from cross-domain collaboration. Digital modernization paired with operational integration is a common example, as is capital restructuring aligned with geographic expansion. Each combination may be individually sound. The audit ensures that their structural interaction is examined before they converge into shared architecture. Benefits are visible and deadlines create momentum. Once implementation begins, reversal becomes difficult and expensive. The audit requires structural examination before that momentum takes hold, not after it has.

Before approving a material initiative, governance must be able to answer a specific set of structural questions.

What does this decision establish as Primary, and what independence does it narrow, consolidate, or remove?

If the initiative becomes central to operations, does a differentiated and funded Alternate remain viable, or has optionality been assumed rather than deliberately engineered?

Have shared enabling inputs, digital, geographic, financial, logistical, or organizational, increased across domains that previously operated independently, and has cross-domain alignment introduced new coupling between tiers?

If simultaneous stress were applied, would failure pathways that were once separate now unify, increasing structural density under load?

Who holds decisive authority as systems narrow, and do escalation thresholds remain explicit and preserved?

Do liquidity flexibility and capital deployment pathways remain clear and functional under stress?

Does the decision expand maneuverability or narrow the institution's structural posture over time?

These aren't hypothetical questions. They're the structural examination that governance owes to every material decision before it becomes architecture.

Boards carry fiduciary responsibility for continuity as well as performance. The Executive Decision Audit provides a record of disciplined examination, demonstrating that independence, correlation, and authority clarity were considered before structure shifted. That record matters not only for defensibility after disruption but for the quality of the decisions themselves. Structural examination before commitment strengthens governance by ensuring that what gets approved can actually be sustained under the conditions it will eventually face.

A proposal that reshapes architecture without articulating its structural implications is incomplete, regardless of how financially attractive, strategically compelling, or operationally sound it appears. That incompleteness isn't visible during approval. It becomes visible when stress arrives and the organization discovers that the architecture it approved can't sustain the conditions it was designed to operate in.

The Executive Decision Audit closes that gap by ensuring that the structural consequences of decisions are examined before they accumulate into exposure. It gives governance a documented record demonstrating that survivability was examined before commitment was made. In environments where regulators, investors, and stakeholders increasingly examine not just outcomes but the quality of the decisions that produced them, that demonstration matters.

CHAPTER 15

Anchored Expansion

Growth and structural discipline are not competing priorities. The assumption that resilience constrains ambition is one of the most persistent misunderstandings in governance, and it tends to surface precisely when an organization is considering its most consequential expansion decisions.

The Executive Decision Audit established a governance discipline for material decisions. Anchored expansion applies that same discipline specifically to growth, asking not whether to advance but whether the architecture supporting that advance has been examined for structural consequence before commitment is made.

Most expansion decisions are evaluated well at the surface. Financial return is modeled. Operational feasibility is assessed. Regulatory implications are reviewed. Competitive positioning is analyzed. Risk committees examine probability and impact across defined categories. Each group fulfills its responsibility competently. What frequently goes unexamined is how the expansion reshapes the institution's structural architecture across tiers, and whether that reshaping compresses the independence that fallback planning depends on.

Anchored expansion addresses that gap directly, applying structural examination to growth decisions before they're approved rather than discovering their consequences after they've hardened into architecture.

When a new initiative becomes central to operations, it becomes Primary. Everything that was previously Primary either remains Primary alongside it, gets displaced, or gets absorbed into a more concentrated architecture. That shift happens whether it's examined or not, and if it isn't examined deliberately, the organization discovers the consequence under stress rather than during planning.

Anchored expansion requires that the layered evaluation that PACE demands of existing architecture be applied equally to growth decisions before they're approved. That means examining expansion not only through the Primary lens of performance projection but through each tier in sequence.

The examination runs through each tier in sequence. At the Primary level: which enabling inputs does the expansion concentrate, which dependencies does it deepen, and what was previously distributed that now converges? At the Alternate level: does the expansion fail independently under stress, or does it introduce new coupling that wasn't present before? An Alternate that depends on the same enabling inputs as the new Primary isn't an Alternate. It's a parallel exposure. At the Contingency level: what simplifies if the initiative underperforms or encounters conditions outside its design parameters, and can the architecture degrade intentionally without losing core mission? At the Emergency level: where does authority concentrate if expansion coincides with systemic stress, which capital channels remain insulated, and how is leadership continuity preserved under simultaneous pressure?

Through this layered evaluation, structural consequences become visible earlier. Assumptions get tested across tiers rather than against a single performance projection. Exposure shifts surface before they accumulate. And something else often happens: opportunity appears.

Structural evaluation reveals what rigid optimization conceals. When leadership examines an expansion through the PACE lens, they frequently discover secondary revenue pathways that weren't visible in the original business case. They find leaner operating models that reduce dependency density while preserving capability. They identify modular architectures that accelerate innovation by insulating experiments from core operations. They see assets that can serve multiple roles across stability and stress conditions, producing value in both.

This is the dimension of anchored expansion that purely defensive resilience thinking misses. Structural discipline applied to growth doesn't just protect the institution from the consequences of its own ambition. It reveals the full structural potential of the decisions being considered, and that revelation frequently improves the decision rather than constraining it.

The organization that examines expansion through all four tiers before committing doesn't move slower than the organization that doesn't. It moves with greater confidence because its architecture has been validated rather than assumed. That confidence is genuine rather than performative, grounded in structural examination rather than optimistic projection, and it's the kind of confidence that holds when conditions change rather than evaporating the moment stress arrives.

Governance that anchors expansion doesn't restrain ambition; it ensures that ambition is built on sustainable architecture. The difference between growth that endures and growth that eventually collapses under stress isn't the quality of the opportunity. It's the quality of the structural examination and architectural discipline that preceded it.

CHAPTER 16

Endurance and Obligation

Leadership is transitory. Architecture endures. Most senior leaders understand that asymmetry intellectually and rarely examine it in structural terms before their tenure ends.

Endurance isn't longevity. An institution can exist for decades while gradually narrowing its future through accumulated concentration and incremental drift. Longevity measures time. Endurance measures whether the institution retains genuine options when conditions change in ways nobody modeled. Current performance is a necessary measure of stewardship. It isn't sufficient.

Most leaders accept that responsibility. The difficulty is that structural discipline competes directly with the incentives that govern how leaders are evaluated during their tenure. Efficiency is measured and rewarded. Integration is praised. Consolidation improves margins. Modernization demonstrates strategic vision. Structural insulation, when it works, produces nothing visible. It preserves normalcy. It prevents cascade. It maintains options. None of those outcomes appear in quarterly reporting, and none of them generate the kind of recognition that shapes leadership careers.

The decisions that most protect the institution's long-term structural independence are often the ones that are hardest to defend in the short term, and the decisions that compress independence most efficiently are often the ones that generate the most immediate performance recognition. That tension doesn't resolve itself. It has to be governed.

Structural concentration accumulates through successful decisions that incrementally compress independence in ways that remain invisible during stability. Each decision is rational in isolation. Over time, the cumulative effect of those rational choices can narrow the institution's structural options in ways that only become consequential when stress synchronizes across domains.

Every capital allocation, modernization effort, partnership, and redundancy removal carries a structural consequence, moving the institution toward concentration or differentiation, toward increasingly shared exposure or greater insulated independence. As these decisions accumulate, they redefine the structural boundaries that future leadership must contend with. Boundaries inherited, not chosen, by the people who come next.

That's the obligation. Not to optimize for the current cycle. Not to maximize performance under current conditions. To examine structural decisions honestly against their long-term consequence and to resist the accumulated pressure toward concentration that efficient institutions naturally generate.

When the Primary fails, what survives next? That question isn't rhetorical. It's the governance standard against which structural stewardship must be measured, and it must be answered before disruption demands it. If the answer is clear and demonstrable, governance rests on architecture. If the answer is uncertain, endurance rests on assumption, and assumption may sustain confidence during stability but it will not withstand scrutiny during cascade.

The obligation isn't purely defensive. Institutions whose architecture has been examined, differentiated, and validated don't just absorb disruption more effectively than those that haven't. They retain the structural capacity to act when volatility creates openings that concentrated competitors cannot pursue. The decisions that preserve independence across tiers are the same decisions that preserve the freedom to advance. That's what makes structural stewardship a strategic obligation, not just a fiduciary one.

The PACE Resilience Framework doesn't promise invulnerability. It structures defensibility by ensuring Primary, Alternate, Contingency, and Emergency tiers are deliberately differentiated and validated. Deliberately differentiated tiers make survivability demonstrable rather than assumed. Consistent examination of correlation exposure surfaces vulnerability before compression reveals it. Clear escalation thresholds replace response paralysis with disciplined action. When architectural coherence connects boardroom deliberation to operational execution, all of those conditions hold simultaneously, and resilience becomes institutional rather than episodic. That's when resilience becomes a decision.

Resilience is an ethical commitment to continuity. It acknowledges that favorable conditions are not permanent and that volatility is cyclical. It insists that independence be preserved deliberately rather than assumed to endure. It requires that each generation of leadership examine the structural legacy it will leave rather than simply the performance record it will claim.

Stewardship isn't abstract. It's the decision to examine structure before compression reveals its weakness, and to preserve structural independence across escalating tolerance thresholds rather than allow drift to define the institution's limits.

Endurance doesn't emerge from aspiration. It emerges from architecture deliberately examined, differentiated, and validated over time. It emerges when boards require structural clarity as routinely as financial clarity, when executive teams align ambition with tier independence rather than assume past performance guarantees insulation, and when operational leaders understand not only what they are building but how it behaves under strain.

In volatile environments, institutions are judged by how they behave when correlation emerges, when stress synchronizes, and when assumptions are tested across domains simultaneously. In those moments, architecture speaks louder than intention.

The leaders who built it may be long gone. The architecture they chose remains.

THE PATTERN

Over the course of my career I have watched the same structural behavior repeat itself across utilities, transportation systems, financial institutions, healthcare networks, energy infrastructure, public agencies, and private enterprise. It has appeared in regional disruptions and in global crises. I have seen it in advanced economies and in developing markets, in conflict-affected regions and in stable ones, across multiple continents and across decades of work.

The sector changes. The geography changes. The context changes. The structural behavior does not.

In nearly every case, the institutions I observed believed they were prepared. Plans had been practiced, backups were funded, and response teams were trained. Confidence wasn't unfounded and competence was genuinely present. What was missing was structural depth, not capability.

Consequence modeling rarely extended far enough into correlated exposure, and mitigation planning addressed the direct event while leaving collateral concentration unexamined. Redundancy was presumed to equal independence, and performance history was treated as evidence of durability. Escalation authority was documented but never structurally stress-tested against the conditions it would actually face.

When disruption remained isolated, those assumptions held. When stress synchronized across systems, or cascaded through compounding inputs, architecture stopped being theoretical and became determinative. The depth of consequence exceeded what had been anticipated, and cascade pathways were more tightly coupled than anyone had modeled. Recovery depended on the same enabling inputs that stress had already compromised, and mitigation strategies proved narrower than designed because they had been designed to overcome a different kind of failure.

This pattern results from fragmented evaluation, not negligence or incompetence. Organizations rigorously assess risk, performance, and compliance. What they rarely assess with equal rigor is how systems fail together, and whether structural independence has been preserved across escalating tolerance thresholds.

The lesson repeats across regions and sectors. Preparation confirms readiness within anticipated conditions. Structure determines what survives when those conditions are exceeded. Institutions that endure are those whose Alternates remain meaningfully differentiated, whose Contingency simplifies rather than collapses, and whose Emergency authority is clear before compression demands it.

That difference is rarely dramatic at first. It becomes visible only when correlation emerges and assumptions are tested simultaneously across domains. In those moments, architecture speaks through decision velocity, authority clarity, preserved maneuverability, and the absence of cascade.

The pattern itself is straightforward. Concentration accumulates quietly. Independence must be preserved deliberately. Stewardship requires examination before compression reveals weakness.

Institutions that embed this discipline move with confidence that is grounded rather than assumed. Those that don't rely on performance history that may mask untested vulnerabilities and fail to repeat under synchronized strain.

The future will not be less complex. Integration will deepen, technology will converge, and capital will concentrate and disperse in cycles. Environmental, geopolitical, and economic volatility will continue to intersect in ways that no planning model fully anticipates.

The question is whether institutions will have preserved the structural independence necessary to navigate disruption when it arrives, not whether they can predict its form.

The pattern reveals the answer. It always has.

APPENDIX

Glossary and Technical Definitions

The terms defined here carry specific meaning throughout the manuscript. Precision in language supports precision in governance, and the definitions that follow are intended to ensure that the framework's application remains consistent whether it is being used in a boardroom, an executive review, or an operational planning context.

THE PACE TIERS

The four tiers of the PACE Resilience Framework are the framework's foundational architecture. They are defined here as a grouped set because their meaning is interdependent. Each tier is defined in relation to the others, and the structural logic of the framework depends on understanding how they function together under escalating compression.

Primary (PACE-RF)

The principal operating pathway upon which normal performance depends, typically optimized for efficiency within standard tolerance ranges. The Primary is where exposure accumulates most quietly, through incremental modernization, consolidation, and integration decisions that individually appear sound but collectively compress independence across tiers.

Alternate (**PACE-RF**)

A deliberately differentiated secondary pathway that sustains essential function when the Primary exceeds its tolerance threshold. An Alternate must be viable, structurally independent in at least one critical enabling input, and funded where required. Redundancy that shares the same enabling inputs as the Primary is not an Alternate. It is parallel exposure.

Contingency (**PACE-RF**)

A simplified operating mode activated when both Primary and Alternate exceed tolerance thresholds. Contingency preserves essential function while intentionally reducing dependency density and structural complexity. Contingency is not a diminished Primary. It is a deliberate contraction designed to preserve core mission when more capable tiers are no longer viable.

Emergency (**PACE-RF**)

The final containment tier within PACE, characterized by concentrated authority, simplified institutional posture, and predefined capital activation under severe impairment. Emergency posture preserves core mission and governance continuity when layered stress threatens institutional viability. It is not improvisation. It is disciplined contraction defined before compression accelerates.

GLOSSARY

Applied Governance Lens

A governance examination applied to material decisions before approval. It evaluates tier independence, concentration risk, authority clarity, and survivability under compression, ensuring that structural consequence is examined before decisions harden into architecture.

Architectural Coherence

Alignment across systems, authority, and resources such that decisions do not unintentionally compress independence across tiers. Architectural coherence is not a static condition. It requires periodic revalidation as the institution evolves.

Authority Architecture

The deliberate design of decision rights, escalation thresholds, and capital activation pathways that determine how authority functions as structural tolerance narrows. Authority architecture must be defined before compression occurs, not negotiated while it is underway.

Capital Activation

The deployment of financial resources under stress conditions. Structural resilience requires capital activation pathways that remain clear, insulated where necessary, and executable under compression.

Cascading Failure

A sequence of failures in which the impairment of one system accelerates the impairment of adjacent systems through shared dependencies, producing consequences that exceed what any single failure would have generated in isolation. Cascade is not an event. It is a structural condition that emerges when tiers share enabling inputs.

Compression

The simultaneous narrowing of information clarity, decision time, operational flexibility, and authority distribution under stress. Compression reveals structural density, shared dependencies, and tolerance limits that stable conditions conceal.

Compression Commonality

The condition in which otherwise distinct risks unify under stress due to shared dependencies, producing simultaneous degradation across tiers. Compression commonality is the structural mechanism through which Correlation Risk becomes consequential.

Compression Point

A shared enabling input or dependency upon which multiple tiers rely. Compression points are the structural fault lines where synchronized stress triggers cascading degradation. They are rarely visible during stability and typically become apparent only when stress reveals them.

Correlation Risk

The condition in which multiple systems or domains rely on shared enabling inputs, increasing the likelihood of simultaneous disruption under synchronized stress. Correlation Risk is rarely visible during stability because systems function within anticipated variance.

Enterprise Risk Management (ERM)

A structured governance approach used to identify, assess, and mitigate risk across operational, financial, regulatory, strategic, and reputational domains. ERM evaluates risks individually across defined categories. It is essential and insufficient on its own as a structural resilience instrument.

Executive Decision Audit

A governance instrument applied during material decision-making to examine how initiatives alter structural independence, compression points, correlation exposure, authority clarity, and survivability under stress. The audit is applied before decisions harden into architecture, not after disruption reveals their structural consequence.

Maneuverability

The ability of an institution to reallocate, adapt, or advance under compression without triggering cascade. Maneuverability is not a natural condition. It is the product of deliberate architectural choices that preserve optionality before volatility demands it.

Optionality Preservation

The deliberate maintenance of maneuverability within institutional architecture, ensuring strategic flexibility remains viable under compression. Optionality that is not architected becomes improvisation. Optionality that is architected becomes resilience.

Risk Management Committee

A governance body responsible for overseeing risk posture, evaluating mitigation strategies, and reporting exposure to executive leadership or the Board. The Risk Management Committee operates within defined risk categories. Structural independence across tiers requires governance examination that extends beyond those categories.

Structural Concentration

The accumulation of dependency density within systems or tiers that increases vulnerability under stress. Structural concentration rarely emerges from negligence. It accumulates through successful decisions that individually improve performance while collectively compressing independence.

Structural Discipline Continuum

The range of institutional positions on structural resilience, from reactive and episodic at one end to fully architectural and embedded at the other. An institution's position on the continuum is not declared. It is revealed by how capital is allocated, how procurement is structured, how reporting is framed, and how strategic initiatives are evaluated before they are approved.

Structural Interdependence

The condition in which multiple components rely on shared enabling inputs, reducing independence and increasing vulnerability under compression. Structural interdependence is not inherently dangerous. It becomes consequential when it is mistaken for structural independence.

Structural Shift

A change in architectural posture resulting from a material decision, altering Primary function, tier independence, or tolerance distribution. Structural shifts occur whether or not they are examined.

Tier Integrity

The preservation of meaningful differentiation and survivability function across Primary, Alternate, Contingency, and Emergency tiers. Tier integrity degrades quietly through modernization, consolidation, and integration decisions that share enabling inputs.

Tolerance Threshold

The point at which a system, function, or tier can no longer operate within acceptable limits under stress. Tolerance thresholds are rarely examined during stability because systems perform within expected ranges. They become visible when stress demands what architecture was never designed to provide.

ABOUT THE AUTHOR

James M. Willis is a structural resilience strategist whose work focuses on how institutions preserve independence under stress and sustain continuity when conditions change. Over the course of his career, he has worked across critical infrastructure and complex operating environments on multiple continents, including conflict-affected regions, where failure carries systemic consequence and where stability can conceal structural concentration.

His work draws on decades of operational experience in environments where the consequences of structural failure are immediate and measurable. That experience shaped the core argument of this book: that resilience is not discovered in crisis but structured before it, and that the decisions which determine whether an institution endures are made long before disruption demands proof of them.

He works with executive leadership and governing bodies to examine how their institutions are actually built, where dependencies concentrate, and whether the architecture they depend on will hold when conditions change in ways their planning models haven't anticipated.

RESILIENCE IS A DECISION

www.ingramcontent.com/pod-product-compliance
Lightning Source LLC
Chambersburg PA
CBHW070832160726

48004CB00001B/352